HEALTH LAW'S KALEIDOSCOPE

For my mother and my daughter

Health Law's Kaleidoscope
Health Law Rights in a Global Age

BELINDA BENNETT
Faculty of Law, University of Sydney, Australia

ASHGATE

Published by
Ashgate Publishing Limited
Gower House
Croft Road
Aldershot
Hampshire GU11 3HR
England

Ashgate Publishing Company
Suite 420
101 Cherry Street
Burlington, VT 05401-4405
USA

Ashgate website: http://www.ashgate.com

British Library Cataloguing in Publication Data
Bennett, Belinda
Health law's kaleidoscope : health law rights in a global age. - (Applied legal philosophy)
1. Medical laws and legislation 2. Medical innovations - Social aspects
I. Title
344'.041

Library of Congress Cataloging-in-Publication Data
Bennett, Belinda.
Health law's kaleidoscope : health law rights in a global age / by Belinda Bennett.
p. cm. -- (Applied legal philosophy)
Includes bibliographical references and index.
ISBN 978-0-7546-2631-2
1. Medical laws and legislation. 2. Medical ethics. 3. Human reproductive technology--Law and legislation. I. Title.

K3601.B46 2008
344.04'1--dc22

2007031216

ISBN 978 0 7546 2631 2

Printed and bound in Great Britain by MPG Books Ltd, Bodmin, Cornwall.

Contents

Series Editor's Preface

The objective of the Applied Legal Philosophy series is to publish work which adopts a theoretical approach to the study of particular areas or aspects of law or deals with general theories of law in a way which focused on issues of practical moral and political concern in specific legal contexts.

In recent years there has been an encouraging tendency for legal philosophers to utilize detailed knowledge of the substance and practicalities of law and a noteworthy development in the theoretical sophistication of much legal research. The series seeks to encourage these trends and to make available studies in law which are both genuinely philosophical in approach and at the same time based on appropriate legal knowledge and directed towards issues in the criticism and reform of actual laws and legal systems.

The series will include studies of all the main areas of law, presented in a manner which relates to the concerns of specialist legal academics and practitioners. Each book makes an original contribution to an area of legal study while being comprehensible to those engaged in a wide variety of disciplines. Their legal content is principally Anglo-American, but a wide-ranging comparative approach is encouraged and authors are drawn from a variety of jurisdictions.

Tom Campbell
Centre for Applied Philosophy and Public Ethics,
Charles Sturt University, Australia

Preface and Acknowledgements

During my teaching and research of health and medical law, I have found that the same themes continue to arise, even across issues that seem to be quite diverse: the meaning of individual choice and rights, the relationship between the individual and the community, and the role of law in an increasingly globalized world. These themes arise against a backdrop of rapid developments in medical science, the globalization of health and health law, and the growing acknowledgement of the links between health and human rights. This book has developed out of my quest to identify and analyse these synergies and connections and their relevance to contemporary health law.

As always, my work has benefited from the generosity of friends and colleagues who have read drafts, discussed ideas and helped me to refine my work. In particular my thanks go to Terry Carney, Michael Freeman, Isabel Karpin, Derek Morgan, Patti Peppin, Kerry Petersen, Don Rothwell, Sally Sheldon, George P. Smith II and the anonymous reviewers of previously published work. I would also like to thank the Faculty of Law, University of Sydney for its continued support of my research. Some parts of this book have been presented at seminars and I am grateful to the seminar organizers and participants for their comments and suggestions. I am also grateful to Roslyn Moloney for her research assistance on Chapter 5 and to Claire Deakin for her research assistance as I finalized the manuscript. The manuscript was completed in March/April 2007 while I was a visitor at the Law School at Chinese University of Hong Kong. My thanks go to Mike McConville, Robyn Martin, Alexandra Lo and the staff at the Law School at Chinese University of Hong Kong for their hospitality. My work has also benefited enormously from my interaction with my undergraduate and postgraduate students in health and medical law at the Faculty of Law, University of Sydney. Their continued enthusiasm is always a source of inspiration. I am grateful too to John Irwin, Alison Kirk, Emily Jarvis, Carolyn Court and the staff at Ashgate Publishing for their continued support of this book. Finally, my thanks and gratitude goes to my family. Without their continued support and encouragement none of this would have been possible.

Research for Chapters 1 and 5 was supported by a grant from the Australian Research Council for a Discovery Project on 'Globalisation and Biomedicine: The Harmonisation of Local and Global Regulatory Demands' (DP0452853) (Chief investigators: Don Rothwell and Belinda Bennett). Chapter 1 was previously published as 'Rewriting the Future? Biomedical Advances and Legal Dilemmas'. This article was published in the *Journal of Law and Medicine*, Vol. 13, No. 3 (2006): 295–303, © Lawbook Co., part of Thomson Legal & Regulatory Limited <www.thomson.com.au>, reproduced with permission.

Earlier versions of parts of Chapter 2 were previously published as 'Gamete Donation, Reproductive Technology and the Law', in Kerry Petersen (ed.), *Intersections: Women on Law, Medicine and Technology* (Dartmouth Publishing, 1997): 127–44 and as 'Reproductive Technology, Public Policy and Single Motherhood' in the *Sydney Law Review*, Vol. 22, No. 4 (2000): 625–35 © *Sydney Law Review* and authors; published by Thomson Legal and Regulatory Ltd <www.thomson.com.au> for the Faculty of Law, University of Sydney. I am grateful to Ashgate Publishing, to the *Sydney Law Review* and to Thomson Legal and Regulatory Ltd for permission to use this material.

Earlier versions of parts of Chapters 3 and 8 were published in 'Written in Code: Diversity and the New Genetics', in Michael Freeman and Andrew D.E. Lewis (eds), *Law and Medicine: Current Legal Issues 2000*, Vol. 3 (2000): 189–203. This material is used here by permission of Oxford University Press. An earlier version of this work was presented at the Feminist Legal Academics Workshop (F-LAW) in Sydney, February 1999; as a seminar at the Faculty of Law, University of Sydney, March 1999; and at the Law and Medicine Colloquium at the Faculty of Law, University College London, July 1999. Earlier versions of parts of Chapter 4 were published as 'Prenatal Diagnosis, Genetics and Reproductive Decision-making' in the *Journal of Law and Medicine*, Vol. 9, No. 1 (2001): 28–40, © Lawbook Co., part of Thomson Legal & Regulatory Limited <www.thomson.com>, reproduced with permission, and as 'Choosing a Child's Future? Reproductive Decision-making and Preimplantation Genetic Diagnosis' in Jennifer Gunning and Helen Szoke (eds), *The Regulation of Assisted Reproductive Technology* (Ashgate Publishing Ltd, 2003): 167–76. An earlier version of Chapter 4 was presented as the Willis Cunningham Memorial Lecture at the Faculty of Law, Queen's University, Canada in January 2006. I am grateful to the Faculty of Law at Queen's University for making this presentation possible.

An earlier version of Chapter 5 was presented at seminars during March 2005 at the Faculty of Law, University College Dublin; University College Cork; the Law School, University of Limerick, and at the Faculty of Law, University College London. Earlier versions of Chapter 6 were presented at the Faculty of Law, University of British Columbia in January 2006 and as a seminar in the Kirby seminar series, University of New England Law School in Armidale, New South Wales in May 2006.

The quote on page 77 from *Year of Wonders: A Novel of the Plague* by Geraldine Brooks is reprinted by permission of HarperCollins Publishers Ltd. © Geraldine Brooks, 2002.

Introduction

According to Thomas Friedman (2005), the world is flat. This flat-world phenomenon is part of the third era of globalization that we live in. While Globalization 1.0 shrank the world from large to medium size, lasting from Columbus's voyage to the Americas in 1492 until 1800 and was about countries globalizing, version 2.0, which lasted until 2000, shrank the world from medium to small and was driven by multinational companies (ibid.: 9–10). Globalization 3.0 is, according to Friedman, about individuals working and competing globally and is transforming the world from small to tiny, while simultaneously flattening its playing fields (ibid.: 10). Although this flattening is occurring at a dramatic pace, Friedman argues that flatness is not a uniform phenomenon. For large numbers of the world's people, the world is not flat and, may not become so (ibid.: 461). Many people live in the unflat world where people are too sick, too poor, or too disempowered to enjoy the benefits of flatness (ibid.: 461–94).

While these forces are undoubtedly transforming relationships between countries, businesses and individuals, the processes of globalization are also undoubtedly impacting upon the regulatory laws and frameworks that set the stage for those interactions. Just as globalization reveals a tension between the universal and the particular, so too law is increasingly embedded in global regulatory developments and debates while simultaneously being driven towards increasing specialization and diversification. In general, law is a jurisdictionally-based discipline and it is this focus on the local that often occupies a central place in legal analysis and debates. In the flattening world of globalization, the global takes on a new significance that demands the transcendence of law's traditional local focus.

Health law is not immune from these broader trends. In the past quarter-century, health law has grown out of its infancy and has developed into an area of growing significance. This development has been influenced by a number of factors including the growing recognition of patients' rights within health care (Darvall 1993), the impact of medical science and technology, developments within the discipline of law, and the impact of globalization, bioethics and human rights on contemporary debates about health. Increasingly, health law is about the legal and ethical challenges posed by the complexities of modern life and death. Law is often looked to as the solution to the hard questions of our time and is forced into the role of arbiter and decision-maker for the imponderable (Smith 2006: 15–16). Law faces the seemingly impossible task of finding a path through an ethical landscape that is dotted with quicksand that traps the unwary. In general, our response to these challenges is to turn to the traditional tools of law reform: to seek the views of the community and experts and to craft laws that represent a balancing of the various interests and viewpoints.

This book is about the ways in which developments in globalization and in medical science and technology open new possibilities for our future – both positive and negative – and about the challenges we face in responding to those possibilities. It is a book about the choices we will be required to make as the future becomes the present and it is about the connections and intersections between the lives of individuals and communities within both local and global spaces. In short, it is about the ways that different aspects of our lives intersect with the lives, rights and interests of others to form a rich kaleidoscope of contemporary life and it is about the patterns and connections that we can choose to make.

Chapter 1 sets the scene by arguing that regulatory debates around biomedicine are characterized by a number of common themes. These include the positive and negative possibilities of advances in medical science in areas such as genetics, assisted conception, and stem cell research. On the one hand, there are the potential therapeutic benefits to individuals and communities that will flow from advances in each of these fields. However, these developments also present reasons for caution with fears often articulated about the directions science may take us. Indeed, the dystopian possibilities of the future are a regular theme in popular culture. Another theme is that of globalization and its relevance to questions of regulatory choice in response to new technologies. Finally, there is the challenge of articulating common values both at the local level in terms of the need to address diverse community viewpoints, and more globally as we seek to develop a common language for bioethics. Chapter 1 argues that an appreciation of these issues is essential if we are to be able to respond to new and emerging challenges.

Chapter 2 explores the changing nature of the family in contemporary society through an analysis of rights in relation to assisted conception. Through discussion of the rights of single and lesbian women to access assisted conception services, and changing views over the rights of children conceived using donated gametes to information about their biological parentage, we can trace the impact of new technologies and social trends on the core social institution of the family.

Chapter 3 focuses on debates over cloning technologies. The chapter analyses the debates over reproductive and therapeutic cloning and the argument that cloning is antithetical to human dignity. The cloning debate also reveals the difficulties that exist in crafting laws for new technologies since legislative definitions can quickly be rendered irrelevant if new advances in medical science do not fit within existing statutory definitions. Finally, this chapter questions the link between genetics and identity and argues against biologically deterministic definitions of the body and identity.

In Chapter 4, the themes of assisted conception, genetics and cloning come together in an analysis of the meaning of reproductive rights in a posthuman world. This chapter asks us to consider whether it is ethically acceptable for prospective parents to use preimplantation genetic diagnosis to choose between embryos on the basis of their characteristics and explores the idea of whether there should be limits to choice. The chapter returns to the theme of human dignity, that was explored in the context of cloning within Chapter 3, and considers the whether human dignity is compatible with posthuman reproduction.

The relationship between health rights and health tourism is explored in Chapter 5, which marks a return to the theme of globalization. The ease of international travel opens new possibilities for interaction between citizens of the world's wealthy countries and those of the world's poorer countries. The chapter uses four examples to illustrate these interactions: (1) the global movement of health professionals, both in terms of migration of skilled health professionals from poor countries to wealthy ones, and also the movement of researchers to jurisdictions with favourable regulatory environments; (2) the relationship between international trade and travel and infectious disease; (3) fertility tourism in which individuals and couples travel internationally in order to access assisted conception services that are unavailable or too expensive in their home countries; (4) transplant tourism in which individuals in need of organ transplants travel internationally, typically from wealthy countries to poorer ones, to receive an organ donation. In each of these examples, there is the potential for individuals to interact across global spaces in ways that may be either beneficial or exploitative. The globally commercial nature of health care services presents significant challenges for countries seeking to regulate these practices and effectively demands the development of global legal solutions.

Chapter 6 explores the theme of the interaction between people in global and local spaces in the context of pandemic influenza. This chapter analyses the threat from an outbreak of pandemic influenza and the role of global preparedness. The role of the revised International Health Regulations as a regulatory framework for international health is also discussed. Finally, this chapter considers the implications of pandemic influenza in terms of individual and community rights through discussion of a reconceptualization of public health law and ethics based on an embodied and relational understanding of public health. In this chapter, it is clear that individuals and communities are linked in the global world and that the health of individuals and communities, wherever they are located, is a common concern.

Autonomy is a constant theme both in contemporary Western thought and in health law and bioethics. Chapter 7 analyses the concept of autonomy in health law. The conceptualization of autonomy as a form of 'self-ownership' is examined through a discussion of whether the body can actually be owned, that is, whether it can be property. The debates around human tissue are contrasted with those relating to the status of embryos derived from assisted reproductive technology (ART). In the case of ART embryos, there is a clear reluctance to apply property concepts to embryos, which are regarded as being worthy of special treatment because of their potentiality to develop into people. This focus on the potentiality of embryos is evident in the debates about stem cells, even though embryos destined for research are destined never to realize their potentiality. At the end of this chapter, I revisit the issue of autonomy through a consideration of the relational aspects of pregnant embodiment and feminist theories of relational autonomy.

Finally, in Chapter 8, I seek to tie together some common themes and consider whether there are common lessons that cut across the diverse range of issues addressed in this book. This book is not a recipe book seeking to provide instructions for crafting the specific detail of legislative reform. Rather, it is a plea for a new, more connected vision of health law which acknowledges differences, diversity and rights, while making connections both within and across the rich landscape of contemporary health law.

Chapter 1

Rewriting the Future?

Medical science has rewritten the future. A relatively small number of discoveries have transformed our ways of thinking about illness, disease, treatments and cures. In the space of one generation, the world around us has been transformed. Caught in a whirlwind of change brought about by the processes of globalization, the speed of the computer age and developments in biomedicine, both the context and possibilities of our lives seem to have become elastic, stretching and moulding into contours that were previously unimaginable. The future shock of our times leaves us with a sense that our communal lives have lost their anchor point, casting us into a realm where everything seems to be negotiable.

It is against this backdrop that governments around the world have pondered the question of regulation: whether regulation of biomedicine is necessary and if so, what form it should take. In many respects, these should seem straightforward questions with achievable answers. Yet in fact, it seems that in many countries regulatory problems have defied ready solutions. Developments in genetic science, assisted conception, stem cell research and cloning technologies, for example, have all sparked major debates about the legal and ethical implications of medical science and have challenged many of our traditional understandings of birth and life. Law reform commissions, parliamentary committees and a range of other organizations have all sought to resolve the seemingly impossible question of the best way to address these issues.

This chapter addresses the points of commonality between new technologies and our responses to them. This is not to suggest that all new technologies have some essentialist, core features, but rather that there are points of commonality in our responses to biomedicine that cut across the discourses surrounding individual technologies within contemporary biomedicine. The approach adopted here involves developing an understanding of the debates over scientific possibilities and their implications (both positive and negative) for human society, the practical limitations to domestic regulatory options posed by globalization, and the challenges of articulating shared values in a pluralistic society. In exploring this approach we may be able to develop both an understanding of the sense of regulatory *déjà vu* that permeates current biomedical debates,[1] and an understanding of the core values that are worthy of legal protection. Furthermore, an appreciation of these discourses and their interaction is vital to an understanding of the regulatory challenges of our time.

---

1 Margaret Brazier has noted (1999: 167) that 'again and again, as new medical developments emerge, we debate the same issues in different disguises'.

The Language of Possibilities

Contemporary debates about advances in medical science are laden with the language of possibilities. Each new advance seems to open a new range of possibilities, with new ways of thinking about our future.

Genetic science is already in the process of transforming our understandings of who we are and why we are the way we are. Major advances in knowledge of the genetic bases of disease have already been achieved, for example, with the identification of the genetic mutations associated with predispositions to breast cancer, early-onset Alzheimer's disease, familial adenomatous polyposis (FAP) and other conditions.[2] The combination of genetic science and computer science opens the possibility of collating vast amounts of genetic information and being able to process and sort that information quickly and efficiently. The storage of information within genetic databases means that information can be utilized for population-wide research on the causes of illness and disease. With this research comes not only the possibility of identifying new genetic contributors to disease, but also ultimately, perhaps, the development of new treatments.[3] Using a form of 'genetic archaeology', scientists will be able to dig down to humanity's roots, tracing mitochondrial DNA back through the generations so as to provide a genealogy of contemporary humanity and new insights into human evolution (Karpin and O'Connell 2002; Tutton 2004).

The quest is on to utilize genomics to explain the human condition, to develop pharmacogenetics so as to target pharmaceutical treatments more effectively, and to understand the workings of stem cells so they can be used to develop therapeutic treatments for conditions as diverse as Parkinson's disease, diabetes and spinal cord injury. The future for modern therapeutics for the human body seems to lie at the genetic level, creating a dynamic between genetics conceptualized in universal terms (a common heritage of humanity) and genetics conceptualized as a blueprint of individual health or disease.

Assisted conception technologies have already reshaped the terrain of the possible. Since the birth of the world's first IVF baby in England in 1978, thousands of couples have used assisted conception in their quest to have a child of their own. The technologies of assisted conception, the ability to store gametes and embryos and the potential for donor gametes to be used at a later date have meant that parenthood has been fractured into genetic and social parentage. This has not only opened up new possibilities for the infertile to have a child of their own, but has also opened up the possibility that the very meaning of infertility could be reconceptualized to include not only the clinically infertile, but also a range of other women, including single women and lesbian couples, who wish to utilize the technology to conceive a child.

Cloning and stem cell technologies represent another frontier of medical science. Both areas are very new, with human embryonic stem cells only isolated in 1998, and the age of modern cloning dating to the birth of Dolly the cloned sheep in 1997.

---

2 For discussion, see Australian Law Reform Commission, (2003: Chapter 2).

3 For an analysis of the legal and ethical issues associated with human genetic databases, see Australian Law Reform Commission (2003: Chapters 18–20).

While both technologies are still in their infancy, and therapeutic applications may still be decades away, these technologies too seem set to transform our understandings of the possible, and therefore to transform our future.

The isolation of human embryonic stem cells in 1998 represented a significant breakthrough in stem cell research. Embryonic stem cells are pluripotent, meaning that unlike other cells in the human body which become specialized or committed to developing into particular types of tissue, stem cells retain their ability to develop into a range of different tissue types. Stem cells have also been identified in adult tissue but to date they appear to be more difficult to work with and less flexible in their ability to develop into different tissue types (House of Representatives Standing Committee on Legal and Constitutional Affairs 2001: para. 2.43ff). The potential to combine some of these technologies with cloning technologies suggests that one day it may be possible to grow new tissue to treat illness or disease.

Each of these technologies seems to offer the potential of a future full of possibilities and hope. Indeed this is the promise of modern biomedicine: to unlock science's mysteries and to develop new and effective therapies for the conditions affecting humanity. This is not to suggest that medical scientists exaggerate the realistic possibilities of their science. Indeed, the limits of current knowledge and the time lag between current research and clinical applications are typically stated very clearly (Braude, Minger and Warwick 2005; Bubela and Caulfield 2004; Byrne and Howells 2003). Rather it is simply to acknowledge that developments in genetics, assisted conception, stem cell research and cloning technologies seem to open previously unimaginable doors and that the landscape beyond, when described in terms of its possibilities, is readily captured in the public's imagination. The language of possibilities is, after all, generally about the opening of those doors and what might, one day, be found on the other side.

Risk and Negative Possibilities

While scientific advances hold out exciting possibilities for the future, the discourses around these possibilities are tempered by concerns over the potential for science to generate negative, rather than positive outcomes, and the need to regulate so as to impose limits on scientific researchers. This then is the flip side to the debates about possibilities: the negative possibilities inherent in technological change.[4] There is a concern that 'mad science' may create a high-tech but undesirable future characterized by eugenics, in which people's options are limited by their genetic make-up, an idea portrayed strikingly in the movie *GATTACA*, or in which reproduction becomes completely high-tech and divorced from natural reproduction, as in the novel *Brave New World* (Australian Law Reform Commission 2003, para. 3.64). As the House of Lords Select Committee on Science and Technology noted (2000, para. 2.2), there is an apparent crisis of trust. While people appear to have an appetite for popular

4 I am indebted to Sally Sheldon for suggesting this way of characterizing the debate around limits.

science, the paradox is that this is accompanied by increasing scepticism about the pronouncements of scientists on science-related policy issues of all types.

The concern over negative possibilities and risk is perhaps hardly surprising given that risk is a central feature of contemporary society (Beck 1992). Beck describes risk society as one in which '[q]uestions of the development and employment of technologies...are being eclipsed by questions of the political and economic "management" of the risks of actually or potentially utilized technologies' (ibid.: 19). A risk society is, as Anthony Giddens points out, not necessarily more dangerous, or riskier than earlier societies, but rather one that is 'increasingly preoccupied with the future (and also with safety)' (Giddens 1999: 3). In the public and regulatory debates surrounding genetics, stem cell technologies, cloning and assisted conception, we can see very clearly the preoccupation with the future that characterizes risk society.

As we live increasingly in a risk society, so the language of risk is used increasingly to guide our decision-making about the future. It is used to make insurance decisions, in actuarial calculations, in financial assessments, to make decisions about safety, and in an array of legal principles ranging from the calculus of negligence in tort law to the precautionary principle in environmental law (Steele 2004). Jenny Steele has argued that the use of risk in decision-making fits in with liberal legal theory's focus on individual autonomy: 'Risk in its positive, opportunity-creating sense is compatible with the richer liberal ideal of the autonomous individual who seeks to maximise his wellbeing through pursuit of a good life' (ibid.: 29). Decision-making on the basis of risk allows us to rely on a vision of the future that can be employed to achieve current goals, yet not only are we unable to determine the future (ibid.), but the future itself seems ever more uncertain (Giddens 1999: 4).

Concerns about risk reflect reservations about the direction in which science may ultimately lead society. At the same time, a range of more practical and immediate concerns have also arisen. While genetic science may reveal the genetic bases of some diseases, there are concerns that the information derived from genetic testing could be used by employers, insurance companies and others to discriminate against individuals on the basis of their genetic make-up (Australian Law Reform Commission 2003). Furthermore, the meaning of 'healthy' has been redefined by genetics, as the line between healthy and ill has been blurred with the creation of a new class of the pre-symptomatically ill – individuals who have a genetic predisposition towards a particular disease but are, and indeed may always remain, asymptomatic. As knowledge of genetics has increased, so understandings of the body and its medical, social and cultural significance, are all in the process of being rewritten.

Just as the discussions of positive scientific advances change over time with each new development, so the discussions of negative possibilities are not fixed or immutable. Within the context of reproduction, the regulatory debates are mediated by a complex array of debates surrounding the nature of the family, the status of the embryo and the rights and interests of children. In some cases, the discussion of negative possibilities appears to reflect concerns that science may accelerate changes that are already taking place in our social fabric. Thus opposition to expanded access to assisted conception services appears to reflect a more general concern about what may be regarded as the erosion of traditional family forms and values in society. The social reality of the contemporary family certainly includes the heterosexual nuclear family but increasingly also includes families comprising single parents, lesbian and gay parents and families of blended relationships arising from the formation of new families through adoption or after divorce. While assisted conception has provided infertile couples with new reproductive options, the claims by single and lesbian women and others to also share in these possibilities has sparked debate over the meaning of 'family' in contemporary society. Public debates over whether access to assisted conception should be limited to heterosexual couples (either married or in *de facto* relationships) reveal the contested meanings of both 'family' and rights to health care in contemporary society.

The potential to link genetic technologies and assisted conception technologies in the form of pre-implantation genetic diagnosis, while simultaneously providing women and their partners with more information on the genetic make-up of their future children, may also appear to take us closer to the slippery slope in which parents choose in advance the characteristics of their children. In the context of these technologies, the question of whether certain forms of genetic testing or pre-implantation genetic diagnosis should be permitted becomes an important but vexed issue for regulatory authorities (Brownsword 2004b; Sheldon and Wilkinson 2004).

The nature and status of the human embryo has also become contested territory. Since developments in assisted conception and embryonic stem cell research both involve the use of human reproductive material for research, the discourses of scientific advance have been countered by discourses surrounding the embryo. Drawing on the belief that life begins at conception, these discourses have argued that such research should not be permitted and have conflated the discourses surrounding protection of the embryo in the context of abortion into the newer discourses surrounding the embryo in the context of stem cell research, resulting in a tangled weaving of the ethical and legal debates across these areas (Dolgin 2003).

Popular fear of eugenics and 'mad science' lend real weight to calls for limits to be placed on science. Some regulatory limits are appropriate to ensure, for example, that research is ethical. Some developments, such as reproductive cloning, the cloning of whole individuals, appear to be so lacking in support within the general and scientific communities that limits may seem appropriate, at least in the short term. In many other areas of biomedicine, however, including therapeutic cloning, pre-implantation genetic diagnosis, and other forms of genetic testing, the placing of limits is less certain and more contested.

Globalization and Regulatory Choice

No analysis of regulatory debates surrounding contemporary biomedicine would be complete without an analysis of globalization. Of course, globalization itself is not a new phenomenon. World religions and medieval trade networks provide an historical perspective on the processes of globalization, although it must be recognized that globalization may take different forms during different historical periods (Held et al. 1999: 13, 17). Yet the globalization of the late twentieth century and early twenty-first century is different from other periods of globalization because of the dislocation and intensification of space and wealth in the current global environment (ibid.: 327).

Globalization constantly dislocates and relocates our sense of space (Beck 2000: 46). National borders appear more permeable and less relevant in the globalized world of international trade and finance, transnational corporations, international media networks and global environmental concerns (Beck 2000: 11). Although the significance of the national appears to fade in significance in a globalized world, the momentum is not all entirely towards an international oneness. Rather, there is a dynamic between the local and the global ('glocalization') (Robertson 1995: 40) that reveals the cultural rewriting evident in contemporary Western society (Held et al. 1999: 373). At the same time as locality becomes globalized, so globalized markets seek to develop local connections (Beck 2000: 46). Within this dynamic Beck argues that 'local specificities are globally relocated and there conflictually renewed' (ibid.: 47). Globalization has been described as 'aterritorial' in the sense that it involves 'a complex deterritorialization and reterritorialization of political and economic power' (Held et al. 1999: 28).

In a regulatory context, this dynamic between the local and the global occurs at several levels: at an international level in the relationships between national and international laws and regulation; within federal legal systems in the relationship between state and national laws, or to use the example of the European Union, between national and EU laws; and at a more micro level in terms of the relationships between individuals and the broader community and in debates over the contrasts between generic (universal) characteristics and rights and characteristics or rights conceptualized in terms of diversity. Each of these dynamics plays a role in shaping regulatory options.

The economic forces of globalization are characterized by the increasing flexibility of movement of people, goods and services. Even health services are available increasingly in more than one locality and patients who are unable to access the health services they desire or need are able to travel to those services wherever they may be located provided they have the financial resources to do so. This phenomenon of 'health tourism', first identified in the reproductive context (Knoppers and LeBris 1991: 333), but now evident across many areas of modern medicine, raises issues of the harmonization of international laws, the value of moral pluralism (Pennings 2002) and the role of law in regulating these activities. Yet the challenges of formulating national regulation in the face of a globalized market for health services are not limited to the area of health tourism. Increasingly, globalization shapes the context of contemporary health care and health law across a wide range of areas (Bennett and Tomossy 2006).

Within the legal sphere, we can see how the development of transnational laws and norms leads on the one hand to a globalized form of law, yet on the other also leads back to a strengthening of the identification with local (national) laws (Chalmers 2003: 547). This dynamic is particularly evident in the regulatory debates within the European Union where there seems to be a heightened awareness of national approaches to regulatory issues within a supranational regulatory context (ibid.). However, this dynamic does present some significant challenges for national (local) regulatory tasks, for at the same time as supranational laws appear to be gaining in importance and the permeability of national borders increases, so too the continued relevance of national laws appears to be increasingly open to question.

Domestic policy- and law-making may be driven by scientific developments that take place abroad. For example, advances in cloning or stem cell research in one country may generate debate in other countries over the scope of existing domestic laws and policies, which may in turn lead to legal reforms. The shaping of domestic law and policy is also increasingly influenced by obligations imposed by international declarations and agreements (Opeskin 1998: 353–4). For example, the development of patent laws at the national level may be shaped by obligations arising from international legal instruments or bilateral free trade agreements (Australian Law Reform Commission 2004: ch. 4). Finally, domestic lawmaking on biomedicine is shaped by the realities of the globalized economy and the need for national economies to remain globally competitive. Domestic regulation is a key factor in scientific and industrial development (Salter and Jones 2002: 326). Uncertainty over the scope of existing laws leaves the public interest unprotected and creates an uncertain climate for business. Effective legal regulation of biomedicine requires the development of flexible regulatory schemes which both protect community interests and are able to respond to and keep pace with new developments in scientific knowledge and medical technology.

In this sense, globalization has the potential to pose significant challenges to the relevance of national regulation of biomedical advances and it is for this reason that an analysis of globalization is so essential to understanding the obstacles to effective regulation of biomedicine.

The Search for Common Values

The increasing relevance of globalization for regulation of biomedicine leads to the question of whether a globalized approach to biomedical issues, and ultimately a globalized approach to law, is desirable or even possible. The desire to develop international harmonized approaches to the bioethical and regulatory issues of contemporary biomedicine is understandable. Many of the issues would seem to be ones for which agreement on core principles should be able to achieved. Knoppers and LeBris have argued (1991: 361) that even if we cannot achieve uniform legislation on a global level, we may none the less be able to achieve agreement on basic principles which 'can reflect our common concern for human rights'. Such approaches raise the question of whether we can agree on claims to universality and a common language of, and approach to ethics.

The rewriting of locality within globalization includes a rewriting of bodily locality and the ways that individuals are situated in the world. There is a heightened awareness of the importance of context and its relevance to the shaping of debates over biomedicine and health law more generally. In the face of this heightened awareness, and given the plurality of modern society, claims to universal values seem increasingly shaky.

Approaches to bioethical issues are undergoing significant change. Roger Brownsword has argued 'that, in place of a two-sided contest between utilitarian and human rights perspectives, we are moving towards a three-cornered contest in which these founding protagonists are joined by a new "dignitarian alliance"'

(2003: 18). This approach is informed by a range of different perspectives, including communitarian and religious views, and together forms what Roger Brownsword has called a 'dignitarian alliance' which is bound together by a shared concern for the protection of human dignity (2004a: 20).

Within bioethics itself 'feminist and race-attentive work has rendered suspect any bioethical approach geared to the generic "patient"' and a new empiricism is challenging traditional principles (Wolf 1994: 397). Discourses around human rights are increasingly playing a key role in the shaping of bioethical issues at the international level (Faunce 2005: 173). There is debate around the place of universal values in a multicultural world (see, for example, Baker 1998a, 1998b; Beauchamp 1998; Macklin 1998a, 1998b, 1999).[5] These developments are indicative of the dynamic relationship between the local and the global in contemporary society. The development of a global approach to bioethics and the need for an increased awareness of the significance of culture have become important issues within bioethics, leaving bioethics at a self-defining crossroads that will shape the future directions of the discipline (Farmer and Campos 2004; Gudorf 1996; Marshall and Koenig 2004; Tangwa 2004).

Some common understanding of shared values and rights is necessary if the language of human rights is to retain its currency (Baxi 1998) for, without such shared understandings, the drawing of boundary lines becomes an impossible task. But such rights, even when expressed globally, always have local context. Thus feminist scholars have reminded the international community of the need for claims for universal rights to expressly address the specific interests of women and children (Charlesworth and Chinkin 2000; Cook 1995; Petchesky 2003). Similarly, there have been calls for respect of autonomy to include an appreciation of the relational and communitarian aspects of autonomy (Nedelsky 1989).[6] Without this richer understanding, claims to global (shared) values that may arise in the context of ethical debates or debates over law reform and medical science will appear increasingly irrelevant.

Perhaps ultimately contemporary approaches to biomedical dilemmas will move beyond simple global or local claims to moral authority and be based on a more nuanced understanding of the complex interrelationships between universal and local values. The manner in which both local and global spaces and meanings are continually de-located and reconfigured in interconstituitive ways by globalization creates opportunities to develop a richer understanding of shared meanings, common values and difference in a contemporary context. This does not necessarily mean that global values have no significance. Rather a new, richer understanding of common values may emerge from an approach in which the limits of universalism are addressed expressly and in ways that reveal an understanding of, and sensitivity to, local contexts.

There is, of course, no easy consensus around the issues raised by contemporary biomedicine. Yet such issues are at the heart of making regulatory choices in a pluralistic society. There is a need for regulatory schemes to 'reflect the reality that,

5 I am grateful to George Tomossy for bringing this literature to my attention.

6 For further discussion, see Chapter 7.

for many reproductive genetic practices, there is no social consensus regarding the potential harms and benefits' (Caulfield, Knowles and Meslin 2004: 415). Despite, or perhaps because of, the lack of consensus, there is a renewed need to ensure that we create the opportunities and conditions for democratic debate around medical science and its possibilities: 'The goal is not, however, to achieve unanimity but to inform the establishment of responsible public policy that is respectful of the diverse nature of public concern and opinion' (ibid.).

It is vital that we continue to articulate the broader values that inform our reactions to scientific advances. The mapping of values on the landscape of contemporary biomedicine is an important task because it will help us to identify those issues upon which there is substantial agreement or disagreement, both locally and globally. Even more fundamentally, the task of articulating values provides an important framework for discursive interaction around the values themselves. What are the values that we hold dear – individually, collectively, nationally and globally – that we may seek to safeguard in our regulatory responses to new science? By explicitly acknowledging the difference and interaction between the local and the global, we can strive towards national and international agreement on key issues whilst simultaneously recognizing that reaching such agreement may be difficult or even impossible.

Regulatory Choices

Advances in biomedical research challenge us to rethink traditional legal concepts and rights. The adequacy of regulatory measures and clarification of key legal issues are important aspects in the commercialization of biotechnology (Chalmers 1999; Nichol, Otlowski and Chalmers 2001). Over the past couple of decades committees of inquiry and law reform commissions in Australia and overseas have debated and made recommendations for legal change on a range of biomedical issues including assisted conception technologies (Gunning and Szoke 2003; Waller 1998), stem cell research (House of Representatives, Standing Committee on Legal and Constitutional Issues 2001), pre-implantation genetic diagnosis (Human Fertilisation and Embryology Authority and Human Genetics Advisory Commission 2001), genetic information (Australian Law Reform Commission 2003), and gene patents (Australian Law Reform Commission 2004).

In the biomedical area the regulatory task is a complex one. While regulatory decisions involve a range of initial questions of whether to regulate at all, and whether such regulation should aim to prohibit or otherwise limit particular forms of research, they also involve a range of additional decisions including the nature of any sanctions to be imposed and any qualifications or exemptions, the balance between public and private law, the choice between direct and indirect forms of regulation, and choices over the regulatory form (Brownsword 2004a: 15–18). The question of regulatory form, for example, presents important choices of regulatory policy (Black 1995) and includes choices over issues such as the balance between legislation and guidelines (Brownsword 2004a: 18; Campbell and Glass 2001; Chalmers 2002).

While the articulation of values is a vital part of making regulatory choices, the regulatory task is complicated further by the logic of individualism and consumerism.

Increasingly, patients are seen as consumers in the marketplace of commercialized health services. In this context, the interface between private choices and regulatory policy becomes an important one (Brazier 1999).

The formulation of laws on the frontier of risk society is not an easy task. The rapid pace of scientific development presents challenges in terms of what Roger Brownsword calls 'regulatory connection' (2004a: 31), that is, the extent to which law meets science rather than trails behind. The tangle of discourses around possibilities, globalization, regulation and risk further complicates the regulatory task. By developing a deeper appreciation of these discourses and the ways that they intersect and at times overlap, we can deepen our understanding of the regulatory challenges we face. It is, after all, in this tangled discursive environment that law finds its place and its role in providing appropriate fora for the dialogue and choices that will shape our future (Lee and Morgan 2001a: 315). If we are to avoid what Derek Morgan has called 'the Red Queen defence: forever rushing to stay in one place' (Morgan 2001: 37) we must seek to develop the fora and opportunities for science and society to engage in dialogue in interactive and meaningful ways that will help us to think about the core values we wish to cherish and enable us to develop the regulatory tools that are adequate for that task.

Chapter 2

Family Limits

The development and availability of the new reproductive technologies have challenged traditional concepts of the 'family' while the meaning of 'parent' has been unravelled into its constituent elements. A genetic parent may or may not be a social parent and involved in raising his/her child; a genetic mother is no longer necessarily the gestational mother, and neither may be the child's social mother. Even genetic parentage is no longer certain. The development of a procedure known as ooplasmic transplantation raises the possibility of a child having three genetic parents. The procedure involves using the nucleus of one woman's egg and donated cytoplasm from the egg of another woman. Since the offspring inherit mitochondrial DNA from the donor as well as from the recipient the offspring would, in effect, have two genetic mothers and a genetic father (Barritt et al. 2001). Of course, the separation of genetic and social parenthood is not unique to the new reproductive technologies. For a variety of reasons, including adoption and divorce, many children have one or more parents to whom they are not genetically related (Charo 1992–93: 22). To a large degree, it is the potential for using sperm and ova in assisted conception procedures that has opened up new possibilities and that has forced us to rethink the meaning of 'parent' and 'family'.

It is somewhat paradoxical then, that while the new reproductive technologies have challenged our understandings of parenthood, regulatory responses to reproductive technology have, at least until quite recently, ensured that the families formed with the assistance of this technology conform to the image of the heterosexual nuclear family. Concern over maintaining the anonymity of gamete donors and the legitimacy of children born as a result of donated gametes, along with the rules restricting access to the technologies, have ensured that traditional notions of the family have not been unduly disturbed.

The use of assisted conception technologies has now become a popular option for infertile people. Figures published by the National Perinatal Statistics Unit have reported that in Australia and New Zealand there were 7,913 live births following assisted reproductive technology treatment in 2004 (*in vitro* fertilization and related procedures) (Wang et al. 2006: 32). In the United Kingdom, nearly 2,000 children are born each year using donated sperm, eggs, or embryos (Human Fertilisation and Embryology Authority 2006: 29). Clearly, there is considerable demand for the services provided by infertility clinics. The enactment in some Australian states of legislation regulating these services,[1] and the provision of public funding for infertility treatment,

---

1 Infertility Treatment Act 1995 (Vic); Reproductive Technology (Clinical Practices) Act 1988 (SA); Human Reproductive Technology Act 1991 (WA); Assisted Reproductive Technology Act 2007 (NSW).

are further indications of government recognition of the legitimacy of using assisted conception technologies as a means of having a child.

Protecting the Family Secret

Legal discourses have always involved a preoccupation with paternity (Smart 1987). Paternity of legitimate children has historically been important in assigning ownership of property and securing succession (ibid.: 99). Historically, the children of a marriage were presumed to be legitimate (ibid.: 104), thus creating a link between children and their fathers and ensuring the support of dependent children (ibid.: 105). Indeed, as Smart argues, it was paternity defined through marriage rather than biological realities which structured the father-child relationship (ibid.: 101).

Assisted conception technologies have raised new issues of paternity, with the focus once again being on marriage rather than biology. At common law, a woman who gave birth to a child who was fathered by a man who was not the woman's husband gave birth to an illegitimate child (ibid.: 106; Warnock Report 1984: para. 4.9). Over time, such stigmatization of the child conceived through donor insemination (DI) came to be seen as unfair since DI children were wanted by their parents and DI was seen to assist the creation of nuclear families rather than undermine them (Smart 1987: 106–107). A distinction developed between the 'wanted' DI child and other illegitimate children, who were presumed to be 'unwanted' (ibid.: 107–108).

The enactment of parentage presumptions reinforces the position of the social father. These provisions mean that, if a married woman conceives using donated sperm with her husband's consent, he is presumed to be the father of any resultant child.[2] Enabling the infertile male partner to appear as the father of the DI child has been seen as being in the interests of the newly formed family. For the Warnock Committee in the United Kingdom, it was regarded as 'consistent with the husband's assuming all parental rights and duties with regard to the child' (1984: para. 4.25).

The presumption of paternity legislatively introduced in response to DI indicates a need to establish clear relationships between men and children (Dewar 1989: 126–7; Sheldon 2005; Smart 1987: 114). However, as Dewar has noted, defining paternity in terms of marriage is a response which 'avoids inquiring into the biological facts altogether' (1989: 127). The maintenance of secrecy, the presumption of paternity and the anonymity of donors in the DI context facilitate the perpetuation of a fiction which obscures the gap between biological and social paternity. By permitting such a fiction, legal discourses support the notion of the family formed by donation as 'normal' (Haimes 1990), while the anonymity of the donor ensures that the fiction will not be exposed since the family's 'non-conformity cannot be manifested in the form of a real, living person' (ibid.: 169).

---

2 Status of Children Act 1996 (NSW) s. 14; Status of Children Act 1974 (Vic) s. 10D; Family Relationships Act 1975 (SA) ss. 10D, 10E; Status of Children Act 1974 (Tas) s. 10C; Status of Children Act 1978 (Qld) s. 16; Artificial Conception Act 1985 (WA) s. 6; Parentage Act 2004 (ACT) s. 11; Status of Children Act 1978 (NT) s. 5D; Family Law Act 1975 (Cth) s. 60H. For discussion, see Gamble (1990: 132); Victorian Law Reform Commission (2005a: para. 2.17–2.19).

Secrecy, including anonymity of sperm donors, has been one of the hallmarks of DI. This is perhaps unsurprising, given the secrecy historically associated with adoption (Achilles 1992; National Bioethics Consultative Committee 1988; O'Donovan 1989). Concerns over stigmatizing the DI child and family, and the emotional difficulties of publicly acknowledging male infertility (Achilles 1992: 28; National Bioethics Consultative Committee 1988: 15–16; O'Donovan 1989: 106–107) have contributed to providing incentives for secrecy in DI. Indeed, some parents may never tell the child of the biological realities of his or her conception (Achilles 1992: 28–31; Haimes 2002; O'Donovan 1989: 106). For those parents, their secret is protected by virtue of the presumption of paternity and donor anonymity. For those who do tell, the information able to be passed on to the child may be limited by rules ensuring the anonymity of the donor. In this context, protecting the anonymity of donors simply seemed like 'the right thing to do at the time' (Haimes 2002: 445). As Erica Haimes has argued, DI presents challenges to traditional assumptions about family forms:

> The main problems are that DI creates three sets of parents who transgress the assumed boundaries of conventional family life:
>
> 1. a mother who plans to conceive a child using the semen of someone other than her husband;
> 2. a father who, even from the preconception stage, plans to raise a child to whom he is not genetically related; and
> 3. another father who plans to have a child with a woman he does not know. [ibid.: 446]

It is this non-conformity that presents challenges. Donor anonymity is, according to Haimes, 'an exercise in "damage limitation" by those who are advocates of DI but who nonetheless perceive potential problems in its use. Anonymity...prevents the non-conforming elements of the receiving family from being exposed' (ibid.).

Ova Donors and Surrogate Mothers

The use of donated ova raises many of the same issues that arise in the context of DI. Indeed, the Warnock Committee concluded, 'It is both logical and consistent that the law should treat egg donation in the same way as AID' and recommended 'that egg donation be accepted as a recognised technique in the treatment of infertility' (Warnock Report 1984: para. 6.6). The Committee made this recommendation after it had concluded that 'since we have accepted AID and IVF it would be illogical not to accept egg donation, notwithstanding the relatively minor surgical risks to the donor inherent in egg recovery' (ibid.).

Unlike paternity, maternity has traditionally been of little concern in legal discourses. In part, this is due to the fact that, unlike paternity, maternity has not been concerned with the status of children (Roach Anleu 1990: 49; Rowland 1992: 268–9; Smart 1987: 115). Since paternity was established through marriage (Smart 1987: 103–104), 'the "illegitimate child", in English and Australian common law, was defined as the child of no one' (Rowland 1992: 268). It is only with the development of the new reproductive technologies that maternity has become an uncertain thing (Smart 1987: 100).

Like their male counterparts, ova donors have been rendered invisible by the circumstances and legal rules surrounding donation. For the ova donor, her role is obscured by legislative provisions in Australian jurisdictions which make provision as to the maternity of a child conceived artificially such that the birth mother is either to be regarded as or is presumed to be the child's mother.[3] These legal arrangements ensure that that ova donor, like the sperm donor, is largely invisible to the infertile couple.

The situation is more complex when surrogate motherhood is considered. When a child is born as a result of artificial insemination in a surrogacy arrangement, the birth ('surrogate') mother rather than the commissioning mother would be the legal mother of the child and, if the surrogate's husband consented to her artificial insemination, there would be a presumption that he, rather than the commissioning father, was the father of the child. This might be the case even if the commissioning parents had provided both the sperm and the ovum; that is, if the 'surrogate' mother was not the child's genetic mother (Millbank 2006b; 214–15; Monahan and Young 2006: 199; Victorian Law Reform Commission 2005b: 22–3). Legislation in the Australian Capital Territory does provide a mechanism for dealing with this by making provision for an application to be made for a parentage order where a child has been born as a result of a non-commercial substitute parent agreement that is, a non-commercial surrogacy arrangement.[4]

Clearly, presumptions as to parentage make the surrogate mother considerably more visible than the ova donor. However, the language used to describe surrogacy promotes invisibility rather than visibility. Even the use of the term 'surrogate' to denote the birth mother, who is often the genetic as well as gestational mother, ensures the 'surrogate' is firmly placed outside the family formed by the infertile (commissioning) couple and gives the whole arrangement a commercial sense (Ashe 1988: 528; Finley 1989: 888). As Pateman has argued, 'The qualifier "surrogate" indicates that the point of the contract is to render motherhood irrelevant and to deny that the "surrogate" is a mother' (1988: 212).

An additional complexity to these issues is that in seeking to choose between mothers in order to determine legal parentage, we may risk losing sight of the social context that gives motherhood meaning. As Ilana Hurwitz points out:

> Motherhood has functional components: genetic, gestational, and the intent to rear a child. The functional components are meaningless, however, without the child herself. Motherhood is also an identity, a complementary form of identity. A woman alone is not a mother...It is the symbiotic connection between mother and child that differentiates motherhood from womanhood. [2000: 129]

---

3 Status of Children Act 1996 (NSW) s. 14; Status of Children Act 1974 (Vic) s. 10E; Family Relationships Act 1975 (SA) ss. 10C, 10E; Status of Children Act 1974 (Tas) s. 10C; Status of Children Act 1978 (Qld) s. 17; Artificial Conception Act 1985 (WA) s. 5; Parentage Act 2004 (ACT) s. 11; Status of Children Act 1978 (NT) s. 5C; Family Law Act 1975 (Cth) s. 60H. For discussion see Monahan and Young 2006: 189–91.

4 Parentage Act 2004 (ACT) ss. 23–31.

Identifying the Gamete Donor

The anonymity of donors in assisted reproductive technology (ART) raises important issues about the rights and interests of the various parties involved: the donor, the recipient couple and the child born as result. Anonymity of the sperm donor is generally regarded as being in the interests of the infertile couple, but also of the donor himself. Several developments combined to turn the tide from secrecy to openness in DI. Firstly, a growing trend of openness to individuals who were adopted as children being able to access information about their birth parents had flow-on effects for debates about the rights of DI children to information about biological parentage. The interests that the infertile couple and the donor may have in maintaining anonymity and secrecy and the interests that the child may have in knowledge of the fact of DI and identification of the donor raise many issues similar to those raised in discussions about adoption (Haimes 1990; 2002; National Bioethics Consultative Committee 1988; O'Donovan 1989). While there are both similarities and differences between adoption and assisted conception, the knowledge acquired from experiences with adoption does appear highly relevant to the new reproductive technologies (Haimes 1988). Secondly, there was a growing recognition of the rights of the child, fuelled by emerging human rights discourses, including the United Nations Convention on the Rights of the Child, which focused on the rights of children as deserving of protection (Petersen 2006: 155–7; Tobin 2004). Finally, a growing social acceptance of assisted conception procedures has meant that their use was no longer seen as extraordinary and the imperative towards secrecy has lessened.

In the wake of these developments, attention has turned to the provision of information to donor offspring about their biological parentage (see, for example, Daniels and Thorn 2001; Lycett et al. 2004; McGee, Brakman and Gurmankin 2001; McWhinnie 2001; Patrizio, Mastroianni and Mastroianni 2001). Despite the focus on openness and disclosure of information to the DI offspring, much of the international literature indicates that parents often do not tell their children about their biological parentage (Infertility Treatment Authority 2006: 3). Concerns have also been expressed about the willingness of donors to donate their gametes if they are unable to do so on an anonymous basis.

In Sweden, where laws permitting donor offspring access to identifying information about sperm donors have been in place since 1985, a study of the 194 couples who had conceived a DI child during the period 1985–97 revealed that 89 per cent of respondents (an 80 per cent response rate) had not told their child about his or her biological origins (Gottlieb, Lalos and Lindblad 2000). Eleven per cent of respondents had told their child (with the majority of these families telling the child at a mean age of 5.5 years) and 59 per cent of couples had told someone else. While some families had not made a decision on whether to tell the child, 28 families (28 out of 132) had decided not to tell the child.

In the Netherlands in 2004, a new law was introduced to provide donor offspring of 12 years and over with a right to access non-identifying information about the donor and for offspring 16 years or over there is a right of access to identifying information about the donor (Janssens et al. 2006). The anonymity of donors who had donated gametes before 2004 on an anonymous basis is maintained (ibid.: 854).

Information about donor conceptions is kept in a central register and doctors are obliged to report the required details to the foundation with oversight of the register following conception with donated gametes (ibid.: 853). Prior to the introduction of the new law, a dual system for DI operated in the Netherlands. Under this dual system, donors could opt to be identifiable or could choose to remain anonymous. There was also a small number of identified donors who were donating to someone they knew (ibid.: 852–4). The impact of Dutch public debate over gamete donation and anonymity has been marked: 'During the last 15 years, the period of debate on the removal of donor anonymity, the number of donors dropped by a factor of three, as a result of diminished recruitment of A-donors [anonymous]' (ibid.: 854). Furthermore, in the past 15 years, donor shortages, the introduction of new government controls, and poor financial reimbursement for DI all contributed to a 50 per cent reduction in the number of sperm banks (ibid.: 855).

In Britain, there have also been changes to the law. Since April 2005, anonymous donations of gametes and embryos have not been used, except in limited circumstances, and once they reach the age of 18, children conceived using donated gametes are able to apply for access to non-identifying information about the donor (Human Fertilisation and Embryology Authority 2006: 30). Identifying information is available if the donor registered after 1 April 2005 (ibid.: 30). Since the British laws only came into operation in 2005, it will 2023 before any of the donor-conceived children are old enough to seek identifying information about their biological parentage. In a recent review of the Human Fertilisation and Embryology Act, the British government indicated its intention to 'recognise in law some reciprocal rights of donors, and to widen access in relation to consanguinity' (Department of Health (UK) 2006: para. 2.58). The government indicated its intention to provide donor-conceived children with a right, at age 18, to find out if they have any donor-conceived siblings (ibid.).

Of Australia's six states and two territories only four – Victoria, South Australia, Western Australia and New South Wales – have legislation which specifically regulates the provision of assisted conception services.[5] In other states and territories, clinical practices are regulated by the accreditation requirements of the Fertility Society of Australia and by guidelines published by the National Health and Medical Research Council (NHMRC). The NHMRC's *Ethical Guidelines on the Use of Assisted Reproductive Technology in Clinical Practice and Research* provide a strong commitment to disclosure of information in the context of gamete donation. The *Guidelines* provide that clinics should not use donated gametes in assisted conception programmes unless the donor has agreed to the release of identifying information to his or her offspring (NHMRC 2007a: para. 6.1). The *Guidelines* clearly rest on principles of openness, stating:

> 6.1.1 Clinics should help potential gamete donors to understand and accept the significance of the biological connection that they have with the persons conceived using their gametes.

5 Infertility Treatment Act 1995 (Vic); Reproductive Technology (Clinical Practices) Act 1988 (SA); Human Reproductive Technology Act 1991 (WA); Assisted Reproductive Technology Act 2007 (NSW).

> Donors should be advised that the persons conceived are entitled to knowledge of their genetic parents and siblings.
>
> 6.1.2 Clinics should help prospective recipients to understand the significant biological connection that their children have with the gamete donor. Recipients should be advised that their children are entitled to knowledge of their genetic parents and siblings; they should therefore be encouraged to tell their children about their origins.

In Victoria, the Infertility Treatment Authority maintains two registers of information about gamete donors and their offspring.[6] The first register, known as the 1984 Central Register, was established pursuant to the Infertility (Medical Procedures) Act 1984 (Vic), and covers births from 1 July 1988 where the donor consented to the use of his or her gametes or embryo between 1 January 1988 and 1 January 1998. The second register is the 1995 Central Register. This register was established under the Infertility Treatment Act 1995 (Vic), which replaced the earlier Victorian legislation, and covers all births from donated gametes or embryos since 1 January 1998. Donors, donor offspring and their parents can obtain access to non-identifying information about each other. Access to identifying information is available, on written application to the Infertility Treatment Authority. However, identifying information is only released if the person to whom the information relates has given written consent to the release of identifying information. Where the person concerned is below the age of 18 years, the Authority must obtain the consent of the offspring's parents or guardian. Counselling of the parties is provided in cases of release of identifying information.

For the children who were conceived using donated sperm and who are now turning 18 years old, the rules relating to disclosure are about to be tested. The first of the children covered by the provisions relating to children born since 1 July 1988 turned 18 during 2006 (Nader 2006). If their donor wants to make contact with them, they may receive a letter from the Infertility Treatment Authority requesting their consent. If their parents have not told them about the circumstances of their conception, this may be the first time some of these young adults realise that they are not biologically related to both of their parents (Nader 2006). As of September 2006, there were over 3,400 births and over 1,100 donors recorded on the Registers (Infertility Treatment Authority 2007).

In South Australia, the Reproductive Technology (Clinical Practices) Act 1988 requires that licensees keep certain specified records, including records about gamete donation.[7] The Act also requires that the identity of a gamete donor not be disclosed unless such disclosure is required for the administration of the Act, to carry out fertilization procedures, or if the donor has consented to the disclosure (s. 18(1)). The Reproductive Technology Code of Ethical Clinical Practice, which is contained

---

6 The information in this paragraph is derived from Infertility Treatment Authority website (Infertility Treatment Authority 2007).

7 Reproductive Technology (Clinical Practices) Act 1988 (SA) s. 13(3). The Code of Practice under the Act, which is contained in the Regulations, specifies details of the records to be kept: Reproductive Technology (Code of Ethical Clinical Practice) Regulations 1995 (SA), schedule cl. 30.

in Regulations under the Act, provides that the identity of a gamete donor can only be provided to the donor's offspring if the person is 16 years or over (cl. 36).[8]

In Western Australia, the Human Reproductive Technology Act 1991 requires licensees to maintain records in relation to gamete donors (s. 44) and establishes a central register for this information (s. 45). Donor offspring can apply for access to non-identifying information about their biological parent (s. 46). For donations made on or after 1 December 2004, access to identifying information about the gamete recipients (the infertile couple), the donor offspring, or the gamete donor can only be provided with the consent of each person who may be identified (s. 49). Information identifying a child conceived using donated gametes cannot be divulged if the child has not reached the age of 16 years unless each person has completed approved counselling before giving consent (s. 49(2a)). A child below the age of 16 years is unable to provide consent but a person with parental responsibility for the child can consent on the child's behalf provided the person has completed approved counselling (ss. 49(2b), 49(2c); see also Tarrant 2002). In Western Australia, a voluntary register has been established by the Department of Health. The register will facilitate the exchange of information between donors and their offspring, although identifying information is only released with the consent of the individual. In addition, the register will provide a mechanism for individuals who donated gametes or were conceived using donated gametes before the Act commenced and before the central register was established to make contact with their donor or offspring.[9]

New legislation in New South Wales will also establish a central ART donor register. The Assisted Reproductive Technology Act 2007 (NSW) will require ART providers collect specified information before they obtain gametes from a gamete provider or before they use a gamete or embryo in the provision of ART treatment (s. 30). ART providers are also required to keep specified records including the identity of gamete providers, the identity of each woman to whom the ART provider provides ART treatment, and the identity of each offspring born as a result of the provision of ART treatment by the provider (s. 31). The Act requires that a central ART donor register be established and maintained (s. 33). Gamete donors, adult offspring of a donor and women who have received ART treatment using donated gametes can apply for a copy of information that is held about themselves on the central register (s. 36(1)). A parent can apply for a copy of information about their donor offspring child that is held in the central register (s. 36(2)). Identifying information about a gamete donor can be provided to an adult donor offspring on his/her application for information (s. 37(1)). An adult donor offspring can obtain non-identifying information about other offspring of that donor and identifying information about other offspring of that donor can be provided if the other offspring have consented to the disclosure (s. 37(2)). A parent of a child conceived using donated gametes can apply for non-identifying information about the gamete donor and non-identifying

8 For further discussion of the position in South Australia see South Australian Council on Reproductive Technology (2000b).

9 Department of Health (Western Australia), 'Voluntary Register: Information About Donation in Assisted Reproduction' <www.voluntaryregister.health.wa.gov.au>, accessed 22 June 2006.

information about other offspring of the donor. A parent may also apply for identifying information about the donor 'but only if the disclosure of that information is reasonably necessary to save the life of the child or to prevent serious damage to the child's physical or psychological health and the information cannot reasonably be obtained by the parent in any other way' (s. 38(1)). A disclosure of identifying information to protect a child's psychological health cannot be made unless written certification that the damage is likely to occur has been provided by a registered medical practitioner with expertise in mental health or by a registered psychologist (s. 38(3)). Gamete donors can apply for access to non-identifying information about children born following the use of their donated gametes in ART treatment and identifying information can be provided about donor offspring if the offspring is an adult and has consented to the disclosure (s. 39).

In New Zealand, the Law Commission listed the principle that 'Everyone should be able to access information about their genetic and gestational parentage' as one of five guiding principles that informed the Commission's review of legal parentage (Law Commission (New Zealand) 2005: 6). The passage of the Human Assisted Reproductive Technology Act 2004 (NZ), which came into effect on 21 August 2005, changed New Zealand's law on anonymous gamete donation (Law Commission (New Zealand) 2005: ch. 10). Clinics are required to provide specified information about the gamete donor and the donor offspring to the Registrar-General of Births, Deaths and Marriages. The Act provides the guardians of donor offspring under the age of 18 years and donor offspring over the age of 18 years with a right of access to information about the donor (ss. 50(1), 50(2)). Donor offspring below the age of 18 years have a right of access to non-identifying information about the donor (s. 50(3)). The donor must be advised whenever access is given to identifying information (s. 50(6)). Donor offspring also have a right of access to information about donor siblings and, provided the sibling consents, may be given access to identifying information (s. 58). Donors may be provided with access to identifying information about their offspring if the offspring has given consent to the disclosure (s. 59).

In addition to the legislative arrangements outlined above, a number of other suggestions have also been raised as possible solutions to the issue of legal parentage in complex situations. These include:

- notifications on or amendment of a child's birth certificate to reflect the realities of genetic parentage. Although this solution seems logical it presents practical issues, including those relating to privacy, given the many occasions on which production of a birth certificate is necessary (Law Commission (New Zealand) 2005: para. 10.44–10.66). The Commission recommended that consideration be given to allowing parents to have a voluntary annotation on a child's birth certificate indicating the child was born by 'donor' (ibid.: recommendation 19);
- granting legal parentage status to more than two persons. While this might be seen to present difficulties in custody disputes in the event of a family breakdown, the courts already deal with similar issues in breakdowns of stepfamilies where a child may have two genetic parents and a social parent (ibid.: para. 6.69).

In three Australian jurisdictions – Western Australia, the Northern Territory and the Australian Capital Territory – legal reforms to provide greater equality and recognition to same-sex couples have been reflected in changes to the laws relating to parentage in assisted reproduction (Millbank 2006a, 2006b). In these jurisdictions, legislation provides a presumption of parentage for the domestic partner of a woman who becomes pregnant as a result of a fertilization procedure.[10] In Western Australia, the law now permits a woman's female partner to be listed on a child's birth certificate as a second parent.[11] This change is significant for it means that lesbian mothers are granted parental status automatically and are not required to go through the process of adoption (Millbank 2006a: 23).

While the presumptions of parentage in relation to gamete donation do obscure the biological reality there are, as the New Zealand Law Commission has noted (2005: paras. 3.19, 6.13), important interests for children in ensuring that legal parentage is clear:

> The rules allocating parenthood protect the child by ensuring that, from the moment of birth, identified adults have legal responsibility for the child and have the necessary authority to protect and care for him or her. Having a legal parent ensures the child's ongoing financial support, which becomes critical where there is a relationship breakdown between parents or should a parent die. [2005: para. 3.19]

While statutory provisions may provide formal mechanisms for children to trace their biological parentage, the Internet may provide an alternative mechanism. In 2005, it was reported that a 15-year-old boy, who had been conceived using donated sperm, had traced his biological father via an online genealogical genetic testing service (Motluk 2005). In the United States, donor-conceived children have made contact with their biological father after the siblings made contact with each other through a donor sibling registry (Glaister 2007). The combination of genetic databases and online services may provide new challenges to traditional concepts of anonymity and privacy in the context of gamete donation and assisted conception.

Access to Treatment

Rules determining eligibility for access to infertility treatment programmes have a gatekeeping role which operates in addition to financial, geographic and cultural factors in influencing access (National Bioethics Consultative Committee 1991). Restricting access to married heterosexual couples ensures that the final products – couple plus child(ren) – match the structure of the nuclear family. As with the issue of donor anonymity, there has been widespread debate in recent years over the issue of access to assisted conception services, with these debates reflecting broader social changes in the structure of the contemporary family.

---

10 Artificial Conception Act 1985 (WA) s. 6A; Status of Children Act (NT) s. 5DA; Parentage Act 2004 (ACT) s. 11(4). For discussion, see Millbank 2006a.

11 Artificial Conception Act 1985 (WA) s. 6A; Births, Deaths and Marriages Registration Act 1998 (WA) ss. 18–22.

In the early 1980s, the Warnock Committee in Britain expressed the view that DI is 'a legitimate form of treatment for those infertile couples for whom it might be appropriate' (Warnock 1984: para. 4.16) and that, 'as a general rule it is better for children to be born into a two-parent family, with both father and mother' (ibid.: para. 2.11). This concern for the welfare of the child was included in legislation with the enactment of s. 13(5) of the Human Fertilisation and Embryology Act 1990 (UK),[12] which provides that:

> A woman shall not be provided with treatment services unless account has been taken of the welfare of any child who may be born as a result of the treatment (including the need of that child for a father), and of any other child who may be affected by the birth.

It has been argued that the rules governing eligibility for treatment appear largely to ignore the reproductive rights of single and lesbian women (Cooper and Herman 1991; Kritchevsky 1981; Millbank 2006a; Note 1985). While the Warnock Committee noted (1984: para. 2.9) that 'many believe that the interests of the child dictate that it should be born into a home where there is a loving, stable, heterosexual relationship', Golombok and Rust point out (1986: 185) that the Warnock Report made no comment 'about the many children who are born into non-loving and unstable heterosexual relationships'. Furthermore, in these days of high divorce rates and single-parent families, many children already have limited contact with their fathers. Golombok and Rust asked, 'Is it really sensible to suppose that the one and half million or so children who are growing up in Britain today without fathers will be damaged by this experience?' (ibid.: 183).

Section 13(5) has been one of the more controversial provisions in the Human Fertilisation and Embryology Act and has 'prompted widespread concerns of principle and practicality' (House of Commons Science and Technology Committee 2005: para. 91) and debate about the role of a statutory authority in making decisions about the reproductive rights of individuals (Jackson 2002; Laing and Oderberg 2005). The provision has been felt to be discriminatory because it treats infertile couples differently from fertile couples, and secondly because the link in the section between the welfare of the child and the need for a father has been seen as an endorsement of a narrow view of the family (House of Commons Science and Technology Committee 2005: paras. 98–101). In a review of the interpretation of the welfare of the child principle, Britain's Human Fertilisation and Embryology Authority concluded that 'there should be a presumption towards providing treatment to those who request it, but that treatment should be refused in cases where clinics conclude that the child to be born, or any existing child of the family, is likely to suffer serious harm' (2005: 6). In its report, *Human Reproductive Technologies and the Law*, the House of Commons Science and Technology Committee concluded (2005: para. 101):

> The requirement to consider whether a child born as a result of assisted reproduction needs a father is too open to interpretation and unjustifiably offensive to many. It is wrong for legislation to imply that unjustified discrimination against 'unconventional families' is acceptable.

---

12 For discussion on the history of this section, see Cooper and Herman 1991: 46–7.

In a review of the Human Fertilisation and Embryology Act by Britain's Department of Health, the British government indicated that it proposed 'to retain a duty for treatment centres to consider the welfare of the child who may born as a result of treatment, or any other children who may be affected' (2006: para. 2.23), but proposed to remove the reference to the child's need for a father (2006: para. 2.26). At the time of writing, the reference to the need of a child for a father would be removed from s. 13(5) of the Act under amendments proposed in the Human Fertilisation and Embryology Bill.

In Australia, access to assisted reproductive technology is governed by legislation in Victoria, South Australia and Western Australia. In other states, the National Health and Medical Research Council's *Ethical Guidelines on the Use of Assisted Reproductive Technology in Clinical Practice and Research* guide the provision of assisted conception services. The *Guidelines* are however silent on the issue of eligibility for access to assisted conception programmes. In Victoria, the Infertility Treatment Act 1995 sets out four guiding principles which are to be applied in the provision of infertility treatment services. These guiding principles are listed in section 5 of the Act in descending order of importance:

(a) the welfare and interests of any person born or to be born as a result of a treatment procedure are paramount;
(b) human life should be preserved and protected;
(c) the interests of the family should be considered;
(d) infertile couples should be assisted in fulfilling their desire to have children.

The welfare and interests of any future child are therefore given primacy over the interests of the family and the infertile couple. This in itself raises some important questions of policy. As Penelope Beem has argued (2004: 4): 'it would appear somewhat incongruous that rights or interests of a "contingently-existing" person could prevail over existing persons.'

The Act requires that in order to be eligible for a treatment procedure a woman must be either married and living with her husband or living with a man in a *de facto* relationship (s. 8(1)). Both the woman and her husband must consent to the treatment procedure before it is performed (s. 8(2)). The Act also provides that prior to undergoing a treatment procedure, a doctor must be satisfied on reasonable grounds from an examination or treatment that he/she has performed, that the woman is unlikely to conceive naturally using her oocyte and her husband's sperm (s. 8(3)(a)); or a doctor with specialist qualifications in human genetics must have performed an examination and be satisfied that if the woman conceived using her oocyte and her husband's sperm, that 'a genetic abnormality or a disease might be transmitted to a person born as a result of the pregnancy' (s. 8(3)(b)). The Act also requires that a woman and her husband be provided with a list of approved counsellors and enough information about the procedure and alternatives to allow them to make an informed decision and must have received counselling from an approved counsellor (ss. 10, 11).

In mid-2000, the Australian community engaged in a national debate over access to infertility treatment services. The debate was sparked by a Federal Court decision in which Justice Sundberg in the case of *McBain v. State of Victoria*[13] held that the provisions of the Infertility Treatment Act which limited eligibility for infertility treatment to women who were married or in heterosexual *de facto* relationships, were inconsistent with section 22 of the Commonwealth Sex Discrimination Act 1984 which prohibits discrimination on the basis of marital status. Justice Sundberg held that, by virtue of section 109 of the Australian Constitution,[14] the provisions of the Victorian Act were inoperative to the extent of the inconsistency between the State and Commonwealth legislation.[15]

The Victorian Law Reform Commission noted in its recent report, *Assisted Reproductive Technology and Adoption* that the *McBain* decision means that 'marital status may no longer be used as a reason to exclude a person from treatment. Women who are single, in same-sex relationships or in unmarried heterosexual relationships where they do not live with their partner on a genuine domestic basis can now access ART if they meet the other eligibility requirements' (2007: 52).

In its report, the Victorian Law Reform Commission (ibid.) noted that the current law is unsatisfactory. Although the Act requires that the welfare of the child should be taken into account when treatment is provided, the Act does not explain how this is to be done. The result of this is, according to the Victorian Law Reform Commission, that 'it is possible for treatment to be provided to people even where it is likely that the best interests of a child to be born will be compromised. Similarly, it is possible for clinics to refuse to treat people on grounds that cannot be objectively supported' (ibid.: 54). Women who self-inseminate may be exposed to communicable diseases if they do not have the benefit of using medically screened sperm, while children may be left without a record of information about their genetic parentage if women travel interstate or overseas to conceive (ibid.: 55). The Commission also noted (ibid.) that the Act's provisions were unfair because they were applied in an uneven manner:

> Some women without male partners will be eligible for treatment in Victoria and others will not. A single woman who has a genetic abnormality which could be transmitted to her child is eligible for treatment. A single woman of 45 may be eligible for treatment because her age has made her clinically infertile. By contrast, a single woman aged 35 who does not have clinical symptoms cannot be treated. These distinctions make no sense and bear no relationship to the concept of the health and wellbeing of the child. [ibid.: para. 55]

The Commission recommended that the marital status requirement be removed from the Act (ibid.: 67), and that eligibility no longer be based on a requirement of clinical infertility, but rather a broader approach based on a woman being unlikely to become pregnant or her risk of having a child with a genetic condition with these factors considered on the basis of the woman's circumstances regardless of her marital status (2007: 68).

---

13 (2000) 99 FCR 116.

14 Section 109 states: 'When a law of a State is inconsistent with a law of the Commonwealth, the latter shall prevail, and the former shall, to the extent of the inconsistency, be invalid.'

15 For further discussion, see Millbank 2006b; Walker 2002.

Under the Reproductive Technology (Clinical Practices) Act 1988 (SA), the legislation limits access to assisted conception services in South Australia to couples who are married or in a long-standing *de facto* relationships (s. 13(3)(b)).[16] In addition, the couple must be infertile or at risk of passing on a genetic condition to a child conceived naturally (s. 13(3)(b)). The Reproductive Technology Code of Ethical Clinical Practice[17] imposes additional eligibility criteria, including a requirement that the couple receive adequate counselling and specified information (cl. 11(4)), and a statutory declaration signed by both spouses stating: that neither of them is subject to a term of imprisonment or an outstanding charge for an offence that may be punishable by imprisonment on conviction (cl. 11(1)(c)(i)), and that neither of the couple has been found guilty of an offence involving violence or a sexual offence involving a child (cls. 11(1)(c)(ii), 11(1)(c)(iia)), and whether either spouse has had a child permanently removed from his or her guardianship other than by adoption (cl. 11(1)(c)(iii)). Since the declaration in *Pearce v. South Australian Health Commission*[18] that the eligibility requirements in the South Australian Act were inconsistent with the federal Sex Discrimination Act which prohibits discrimination on the basis of marital status, assisted conception services in South Australia have been available to single women and women in *de facto* relationships provided they are infertile or at risk of passing on a genetic defect and satisfy other eligibility criteria (South Australian Council on Reproductive Technology 2000a).

In Western Australia, reproductive technology is regulated by the Human Reproductive Technology Act 1991. Individuals are eligible for treatment if for medical reasons they are unable to conceive as a couple, if for medical reasons a woman is unable to conceive, or if a woman or a couple would otherwise be likely to be affected by a genetic abnormality or disease (s. 23(a)). If two people are seeking treatment as a couple, they must be either married to each other or in a heterosexual *de facto* relationship with each other (s. 23(c)). Age must not be the reason for the infertility (s. 23(d)). Prior to the treatment being given, there must be effective consent from each of the participants (s. 23(b)), and consideration must have been given to the welfare and interests of the participants and any child likely to be born from the procedure (s. 23(e)).

Clearly in the context of providing access to DI to lesbian women, there have been concerns over the non-conformity of lesbian couples. There may be beliefs that such couples do not constitute a family, that they are not normal, or that they are not biologically infertile and therefore should be ineligible for treatment (for discussion see Cooper and Herman 1991: 57–8; Somerville 1982: 131–3). There may also be concerns that parental homosexuality may have adverse effects on a child raised in a lesbian household (for discussion see Cooper and Herman 1991: 54–5; Somerville 1982: 133), although research studies refute such assumptions (see Dower 2001;

16 *De facto* relationships must be for the immediately preceding five years or an aggregate of five years in the previous six years: s. 13(3)(4).

17 Contained in the Reproductive Technology (Code of Ethical Clinical Practice) Regulations 1995 (SA).

18 (1996) 66 SASR 486.

McNair 2004; Victorian Law Reform Commission 2007, 32–4; Walker 2002). As the New Zealand Law Commission noted:

> As a rule children fare better in two-parent families than one-parent families, but for each child the outcome will nevertheless depend upon...other factors. Family structure in itself is not predictive of parenting quality, and it is an inadequate proxy measure for child outcomes due to the huge variation in levels of functioning within any one family form. [2005: para. 2.10]

While the published research supports the view that parenting styles of parents of children conceived through the use of assisted reproductive technology are positive, factors that are external to the family, such as social prejudice, reduced social support for alternative family types and reluctance to disclose the full extent of family relationships to others, may result in stigmatization of the family which can in turn have negative consequences for the child (McNair 2004: 19–27). However, as McNair points out, this does not mean that the children conceived through ART (assisted reproductive technology) are victimized:

> These children appear to be remarkably resilient, negotiating the stigma by developing strong peer relationships through careful choice. They are not only aware of their own family diversity, but develop a rich understanding of diversity more broadly. This does not happen by accident. Having made a deliberate choice to have children, these parents are providing an effective and loving environment and equipping their children with skills that build resilience. They are also imbuing their children with the value of acceptance. [ibid.: 68]

Despite the incorporation of the new reproductive technologies into the mainstream, these technologies can still be seen as posing a challenge to the heterosexual nuclear family, as the debate over access for single and lesbian women and access to IVF shows. Single women may require access to IVF if they are unable to conceive naturally. However, even single women who are able to conceive naturally may seek access to assisted conception services such as artificial insemination. For women without a male partner, access to assisted conception services ensures that conception is medically supervised, and that the procedure is performed at the clinically optimal time. Furthermore, and most importantly, access to medically supervised assisted conception provides the woman with access to medically screened donated gametes, thus ensuring that the woman is not exposed to the risk of infectious disease.

The perception of single motherhood as immoral, disruptive and against the interests of children is hardly new. Single motherhood has long been stigmatized. Teenage single motherhood, lesbian motherhood and unwed single motherhood in particular have been stigmatized, with single mothers discriminated against for their perceived immorality for having children outside of marriage (Dowd 1995: 42), for the economic disadvantage of their children (ibid.: 26–35; Fineman 1991), and for the lack of a father in their children's lives (Dowd 1995: 39). Ruth Sidel points out in her work on single motherhood in the United States that single mothers are stigmatized not only for being single mothers, but also for how they came to be single mothers. She points out that single mothers are criticized for divorcing their partners, or for becoming pregnant outside of marriage; criticisms that carry with them the ideas that single mothers are irresponsible, that the women had genuine choices and that they could have made better choices (2006: 26–7).

The stigmatization of single mothers stands in stark contrast to the position of single fathers, who are generally not stigmatized (Dowd 1995: 50). Indeed, as Fineman has argued, the very fact that we refer to 'single mothers' reveals a distinction between other forms of motherhood that are defined by marital status. We do not, after all, refer to a 'married mother': 'It is only the deviant form of motherhood that needs qualification and, by implication, justification' (1991: 291).

This conceptualization of families headed by single mothers as unusual and marginal is reinforced by the focus on fatherhood in debates around assisted conception. While it might be thought that the focus on fathers arises from a concern for the financial security of families and the benefit of a male role-model for children, Sally Sheldon argues that there are two reasons for doubting this. Firstly, if financial security or the presence of two carers was a relevant consideration, then the gender of the parties or their sexuality should be irrelevant (2005: 535). Secondly, the relative privilege accorded to widows in debates around assisted reproduction highlights the fact that 'fatherhood's perceived importance lies primarily in its symbolic function of completing the nuclear family' (ibid.: 535).

While single motherhood is still stigmatized, even that stigmatization has decreased dramatically in recent decades as the increase in the numbers of ex-nuptial births show (Dowd 1995: 43). Changes in divorce laws and trends in divorce have also impacted upon single motherhood (ibid.: 43). There are signs of change. As this chapter has shown, restrictions on access to assisted reproduction services by single women and lesbians are gradually being eased. The increasing number of single-parent families and the growing social acceptance of gay and lesbian couples have led to legal reform across a range of areas, including eligibility for assisted reproductive services (Millbank 2006a, 2006b).

'My Own Child'

Being a parent and having a genetically related child are of course not synonymous. There are a variety of ways in which individuals can act as a parent to a child to whom they are not genetically related. Adoption is one example, while divorce and remarriage or cohabitation present other examples (Charo 1992–93: 2). Yet, for those who wish to have a child, there will often be the wish to have a child of their own and the idea of having a genetically related child will be something quite special.

One of the great advantages of reproductive technology, and perhaps one of the reasons for its great popularity, is that it allows infertile couples to have a child of their 'own' (Overall 1987: 145, 150). The child conceived through reproductive technology can be the genetic child of at least one, and often both, of his or her social parents. Indeed, even if donated gametes are used, the presumptions as to parentage ensure that the child will pass as the child of both members of the couple. Obviously this has enormous appeal for the infertile couple. With the help of some technological assistance at conception, the child is 'theirs' in the same sense that a naturally conceived child is the child of his or her parents (ibid.: 143–51). The parents may experience satisfaction or even joy at knowing that the child is their biological child, in watching the child grow and in seeing the development of family characteristics, such as appearance (ibid.: 154). For women, there may be a wish to experience the biological and nurturing aspects of mothering (ibid.: 147), while men in particular, may feel that it is important to be genetically related to the child (Gaze 1992: 46; Overall 1987: 151). Clearly, many of these factors may motivate infertile couples to seek the assistance of reproductive technology. The desire to maintain the family's appearance of 'normality' may also help to explain the complexity and challenges associated with disclosure of information in the context of gamete donation. Indeed, it has been argued that the 'literature on parents telling their children that they were donor-conceived (and on associated matters such as donor anonymity) presents a picture of complex human relationships and multi-layered meanings of genes, infertility, identity, and family' (Infertility Treatment Authority 2006: 9).

While some feminists have been critical of the new reproductive technologies (see discussion in Morgan 2001: ch. 5), it is also important to recognize the autonomy of women and men who decide to use the technologies and the ability of these individuals to make meaningful choices (Roach Anleu 1997). It is important to acknowledge the interests of infertile women and couples in the use of assisted reproductive technologies to achieve a pregnancy and to accept their interest in having a genetically related child if possible (Sandelowski 1990). Genetic links are important to us. They play an important role in shaping our sense of identity (O'Donovan 1989), and they have strong social and cultural significance (Charo 1992–93). Our sense of who we are and where we have come from is often determined, or at least influenced, by our family links, and our sense of self within a kinship structure. Knowledge of biological parentage is something that is generally valued in our society and it is in this sense that genetic identity can be important. The significance that people can attach to knowledge of genetic 'roots' is apparent when debates over access to adoption information are considered. In recent years, we have seen a freeing-up of restrictions on access to information about biological parentage for adopted individuals. We are also now seeing a easing of access to information for individuals who have been conceived through the use of donated gametes or embryos in reproductive technology programmes. Of course it is not the biological nature of the genetic information, in and of itself, that is generally so important to us, but rather it is the social significance, the meanings of kinship, that attach to that information.

Yet even while we recognize the cultural significance of genetic links between individuals, it is also important to appreciate the normative component inherent in those links. Dorothy Roberts has pointed out the role of genetic ties in defining identity in terms of race and the 'indeterminancy of the legal and social meaning of the genetic tie' (1995: 210). She argues, 'for example, the institution of slavery made the genetic tie to a slave mother critical to determining a child's social status, yet legally insignificant to the relationship between male slaveowners and their mulatto children' (ibid.). It is critical that we be aware of the ways that genetics can be used to ascribe certain characteristics and for these to be used as a means for ordering privilege.

There is a need of course to think beyond genetics and for a greater appreciation of kinship and family structures that are not founded on genetic links between family members. In the modern family, where children may be conceived through assisted conception techniques using donated sperm and/or ova, where parents can divorce and remarry, where there may only be one parent, or where both partners may be of the same sex, it makes little sense for us to limit our understandings of family to a heterosexual couple and their two biological children. Nevertheless, even in the diversity of the modern family setting, knowledge of where one has come from, genetically speaking, whether that be from a resident parent or from a sperm donor, can still be an important element in one's identity. To deny the relevance of genetics for identity seems counterintuitive. To overstate its relevance is equally counterintuitive.

Rethinking the Family

As the discussion above shows, the use of donated gametes has been surrounded by secrecy. The presumption of paternity for the husband who consents to his wife's artificial insemination, as well as the anonymity of the sperm donor, ensure that the husband's infertility is hidden from general knowledge, and perhaps even from the child, unless the couple decide to disclose the matter themselves.

Certainly, one cannot criticize infertile couples for wishing to use assisted conception techniques in order to help them to form a family in which their child is, to the extent possible, genetically related to his or her parents. Nor can infertile couples be criticized for wanting to maintain their privacy in relation to their child's conception. After all, the privacy of the family is still a very strong social norm, particularly on matters concerning reproduction. So, while we must respect the rights and decisions of infertile couples and individuals, we must also be wary of legal responses which reinforce secrecy and potentially make it difficult for children born as a result of assisted conception techniques to discover the identity of their genetic parents. We must also be wary of discourses surrounding the new reproductive technologies which seem to define the family *only* in terms of the nuclear family. There are, after all, many families today that do not conform to this mould. Claims by gay and lesbian couples to be seen as a family have joined rising divorce rates and increasing numbers of single-parent families in their challenges to the nuclear family and the idea that it is the norm. Furthermore, with assisted reproductive technologies we are increasingly facing claims between different categories of parents, as the courts and legislatures address issues such as surrogacy, disposition of frozen embryos and the availability of information about gamete donors (Charo 1992–93: 20). Rather than trying to decide who is, or is not, a child's parent we could, as Charo suggests, recognize that a child may have more than two parents (ibid.: 20).

The stigmatization of single motherhood occurs in a context that sees the family conceptualized in terms of the sexual bond between heterosexual adults (Fineman 1992: 663). Even in calls for a definition of the family that includes non-traditional unions, the sexual bond between adults is central (ibid.: 663). As Martha Fineman has noted, 'The form of argument is by analogy. Nontraditional unions are equated with the paradigmatic relationship of heterosexual marriage' (ibid.: 663). However, we could, as Fineman suggests, conceptualize the family differently:

> Instead, it might begin with the premise that the basic family unit consists of mother and child. Although this is the family form experienced for significant time periods by many women and children in our society, it has never been accepted as a positive ideological or rhetorical alternative to the sexual family. A woman and her children 'alone' are considered an *incomplete*, and thus a deviant unit. They are identified as a source of pathology, the generators of problems such as poverty and crime. [ibid.: 664, original emphasis]

It is this focus on the bond between adults as the basis for defining the family that facilitates the stigmatization of single motherhood.

The debate over single women having access to IVF and related services is not simply a debate over reproductive technology. It is rather a debate over the very meanings of motherhood and the family in our society. Certainly the family (both its structure and its definition) is in transition. The new reproductive technologies have not created single motherhood. It is clear that these trends are occurring as part of broader social changes, and are not dependent on the availability of assisted conception procedures. However, it is also clear that the new reproductive technologies have presented, and will continue to present, us with new situations and dilemmas that challenge us to define the meaning of family, and the appropriate regulatory framework for assisted conception services.

As Erica Haimes points out, policies about donor anonymity are significant because of 'their ramifications for a number of key relationships between individuals...and for a number of key relationships within and between major social institutions' (2002: 447). The challenge presented by reproductive technology must surely be to respect the rights of women receiving ART, gamete donors, and children born following ART, while critically evaluating and seeking to transcend the narrow confines of the definition of 'family' within which reproductive technology operates.

Chapter 3

Written in Code

In July 1996 in Scotland, Dolly the sheep was born. The announcement of Dolly's birth in early 1997 attracted international scientific and media attention – not the usual way of marking the birth of one more sheep in the world. However, Dolly was different. Born at the Roslin Institute in Scotland, Dolly was a clone. With the birth of one sheep, cloning moved from the realm of futuristic science fiction, into the realm of the present and possible. The furore that followed was, in many ways predictable, for Dolly's birth appeared to open a Pandora's box of ethical dilemmas about the cloning of human beings. International concern over the potential for human cloning motivated governments and other bodies to consider its implications. Overwhelmingly, cloning of whole individuals has been condemned.

While the significance of Dolly's birth must not be understated, it is also important to see debates over cloning within the broader context of debates over developments in genetic science generally. It was in 1953 that James Watson and Francis Crick unlocked the key to modern genetics when they discovered the structure of DNA. Since then genetic research has brought discoveries which have helped us to understand the genetic basis of some diseases and conditions and there is the promise of further developments (Bodmer and McKie 1994; Kolata 1997; Watson 2004).

Modern genetic research holds out the promise of a bold new future in which humanity has identified and conquered the genetic roots of many diseases. It also holds out the promise of a successful 'archaeological dig' of human genetics that will reveal humanity's ancestral history through a genetic tracing of the development of the human species (Karpin and O'Connell 2002; Tutton 2004). Genetic science also promises to shed light on who we are, what it is that makes us tick, what it is that makes us the way we are – in short, what it is that makes us human.

Yet while genetics is a potential saviour (saving us from disease), it also appears as a threat that at the extremes appears to be the stuff of our worst nightmares (Annas 1990), such as the prospect, probably more imagined than real, of rows of cloned individuals. The new genetics holds out the promise that through genetics we will be able to determine what we are: a promise that is simultaneously appealing and terrifying. Between the extremes of saviour and horror there are many other concerns along the spectrum about issues such as the meaning of human dignity in the genetic context, privacy and genetic testing, discrimination, and the potential eugenic uses of genetics (Australian Law Reform Commission 2003; Beyleveld and Brownsword 1998; Chalmers 1999; McLean 1998).

Therapeutic and Reproductive Cloning

The birth of Dolly the sheep seemed to have the potential to blur the distinction between science fiction and science fact. Suddenly, cloning of mammals was real. Taking the step from cloning sheep to cloning humans seemed frighteningly possible. The process that led to Dolly's birth truly was an enormous development in medical science. Dolly's birth resulted from the transfer of the nucleus of a somatic[1] cell from an adult sheep, into another sheep's egg from which the nucleus had been removed. The significance of this achievement is that it showed that genetic material could be removed from a differentiated somatic cell (a cell containing two sets of chromosomes), and that that genetic material could be 'reprogrammed' or 'reactivated well into the chronological life of the cell' (National Bioethics Advisory Commission 1997: i).

Works of fiction have long warned of the dangers of attempting to play God by tinkering with human nature. Both Mary Shelley's *Frankenstein* and Aldous Huxley's *Brave New World* warn, in very different ways, of the horrors that can be unleashed when we seek to control the processes of creating human life, while more recently, Kazuo Ishiguro's *Never Let Me Go* tells of a dystopian future in which people's lives are predetermined, with some lives existing solely for the benefit of others. On the big screen, movies such as *The Boys From Brazil*, *Jurassic Park* and *GATTACA* have shown us what can happen if we play with genetics. Dean Bell has argued that these forms of popular culture have 'leaked into the formal policy and legal debates' in two important ways (1999: 218): firstly, by providing 'a symbolic reference to "intuitive" hostility to human cloning', and secondly, they serve as a 'backdrop to many of the rights and interests which, it has been argued, are infringed by human cloning' such as human dignity and the rights of children.

Within the cloning controversy, it is necessary to distinguish between cloning of people (reproductive cloning) and cloning of tissue, often called 'therapeutic cloning'. While much of the debate over cloning has focused on cloning of whole individuals, there is also potential for cloning of human cells for therapeutic purposes. It has been suggested, for example, that cell nucleus transfer techniques could be used for cell or tissue therapy. As the United Kingdom's Human Genetics Advisory Commission and Human Fertilisation and Embryology Authority noted:

> People who have tissues or organs damaged by injury or disease (e.g. skin, heart muscle, nervous tissue) could provide their own somatic nuclei and, by using these to replace nuclei in their own or donated eggs, individual stem cells (not embryos) could be produced in culture. These cells could then be induced (by exposure to appropriate growth factors) to form whichever type of cell or tissue was required for therapeutic purposes with no risk of tissue rejection and no need for treatment of the patient with immunosuppresive drugs. [1998: para. 5.3]

While there are clearly enormous benefits to medical advances of these kind, potential research into these areas is limited by legal regulation of research using human reproductive material. The cloned child could be the ultimate solution to infertility,

1 A somatic cell is a non-reproductive cell.

and cloning may hold the promise of therapeutic uses such as organs or tissue that will not be rejected by the body when transplanted (and indeed this form of therapeutic cloning has encountered less opposition than reproductive cloning), yet it is the prospect of a cloned individual that strikes fear into the hearts and minds of many.

This is not to suggest that the debates over therapeutic cloning have been uncontroversial. Indeed, the developments in somatic cell nuclear transfer technologies have also generated significant debate that intersects and interweaves with the debates over reproductive cloning in ways that muddy the issues across both areas. The intersection occurs because the technique of somatic cell nuclear transfer (the technique used to create Dolly) can be used to create embryos that may be used for stem cell research or other forms of research or alternatively, that may be used for reproductive cloning. The use of human reproductive material for research purposes has its own set of complications, for the debates in this area not only intersect with those around reproductive cloning but also with those around abortion and the moral status of the human embryo (Dolgin 2003). Although the term 'therapeutic cloning' or other terms such as 'non-reproductive cloning' are used as scientists seek to separate stem cell research from reproductive cloning (Lockhart Review 2005: 55), uncoupling these two areas is likely to be more difficult than simply changing terminology.

Cloning and Human Dignity

Reproductive cloning has been condemned internationally (for discussion see Bell 1999; Beyleveld and Brownsword 1998: 678–9). Concern has been expressed over the potential for cloning to undermine the individuality of the cloned child through the deliberate creation of a delayed genetic 'twin' and over the potential for the life expectations and autonomy of cloned individuals to be diminished by the expectations others will have of their behaviour or personality (National Bioethics Advisory Commission 1997: 67–8). In its 2002 report on *Human Cloning and Human Dignity*, the President's Council on Bioethics in the United States expressed concerns over identity and individuality for cloned children. While acknowledging that individuals' identities are not predetermined by their genetic make-up, the Council was of the view that 'our genetic uniqueness...is an emblem of independence and individuality. It endows us with a sense of life as a never-before-enacted possibility' (2002: 102).

The truth about the link between genetics and human health and behaviour is likely to be a complex mix of both genetic and environmental factors. As Erik Parens has noted, 'All behavior results from the interaction of genetic and environmental variables. It's always nature *and* nurture, and nature *via* nurture' (2004: S31). The debates over these issues are central to the scientific and cultural significance that is accorded to information about genetic characteristics. Yet in the balance of the debate over nature versus nurture as determinants for human characteristics, the scales seem to be tipping towards nature. Explanations for human disease and behaviour that are based on genetics are very appealing, since they appeal to our desire for both neutrality and certainty. Yet the focus on genetics and biological determinations of health and behaviour raises new questions about the role of individuals. Within this complex mix of genes and environment, how much of what we are is within our power to change? There is a risk that individual agency and social and cultural influences will fade into the background as biological coding takes on a new prominence. In addition to raising new questions about human freedom and individual agency, behavioural genetics will also raise questions about human equality:

> Would it affect our understanding of moral equality if we learned that genetic differences help to explain why we behave and appear differently, if we learned, for example, that some individuals are genetically predisposed to antisociality or hypergenerosity, alcoholism or teetotaling, low intelligence or high? [Parens 2004: S1]

The identification of certain behaviour as genetic in origin further reinforces notions of genetic health and normality. The loaded nature of genetic information and the social and legal consequences of that information are areas that the new genetics has opened up and that we are only now beginning to tackle.

The limits of the notion that someone's identity is genetically determined and that cloning means that an individual's identity is already predefined, quickly become apparent if we consider the case of identical twins. Identical twins have the same DNA since they are the product of the splitting of one fertilized egg. Yet while we often accept that there is a special bond between twins, we do not necessarily expect them to have identical personalities, or identical lives. Yet in the cloning debate, little account seems to be made for the impact of social and environmental factors in the development of personality. It is also true that we do not regard the lives of identical twins as somehow diminished because they have a twin with the same DNA – if anything we regard them as having something extra in the special bond that often exists between twins. In their 1998 report on human cloning, the British Human Genetics Advisory Commission and Human Fertilisation and Embryology Authority referred to the case of identical twins, stating that 'Personhood derives from a humanity that is expressed through relationships with others' (1998: para. 6.1). As the report noted, in the case of identical twins, the existence of a natural clone is not regarded as threatening the identity of the individual. The report concluded that 'the claim that each person is entitled to a unique genetic make-up is a correspondingly questionable assertion. Of itself, it could not prove an adequate ethical objection to human reproductive cloning' (ibid.). The report did note however, that with cloning it is possible to create a delayed twin and that this possibility could present 'novel problems' (ibid.).

Of course not everyone assumes a clone will have a personality that is identical to his or her earlier twin. In most discussions of cloning and identity, there is an acknowledgement of the relevance of cultural and environmental factors in shaping an individual. Yet even where there is this recognition, the magnetic pull of science is very strong, and the tendency to slide towards biological determinism remains.

Other concerns over cloning include the change in social values that will occur in a world where cloning is permitted (National Bioethics Advisory Commission 1997: 69), or for the potential for individuals to become objectified, particularly if the cloned child is brought into existence for the benefit of another person, such as where a bone marrow donor is needed (ibid.: 71–3), or by changing procreation into a made-to-order process (ibid.: 71; President's Council on Bioethics 2002: 104–107). Finally, the spectre of eugenics raises its head in a world where cloning is possible, with parents choosing the characteristics of their offspring (National Bioethics Advisory Commission 1997: 74; President's Council on Bioethics 2002: 107–10). Importantly, the debate over cloning gives us choice over the kind of society we want. The President's Council on Bioethics has argued:

> A society that clones human beings thinks about human beings (and especially children) differently than does a society that refuses to do so...Precisely because the stakes are so high, precisely because the new biotechnologies touch not only our bodies and minds but also the very idea of our humanity, we should ask ourselves how we as a society want to approach questions of human dignity and flourishing. [2002: 113]

The United States National Bioethics Advisory Commission concluded in its June 1997 report on human cloning that 'at this time it is morally unacceptable for anyone in the public or private sector, whether in a research or clinical setting, to attempt to create a child using somatic cell nuclear transfer cloning' (1997: 108). The Commission was of the view that at this time cloning was not safe for human use and furthermore, that the ethical concerns over cloning required 'much more widespread and careful public deliberation' before cloning is used (ibid.). The Commission also recommended the enactment of federal legislation, with a sunset clause, to prohibit attempts at creating a child through somatic cell nuclear transfer cloning, either in a research or a clinical setting (ibid.: 109). In its 2002 report the President's Council on Bioethics recommended the enactment of a ban on reproductive cloning and a moratorium on the use of cloning in biomedical research. The Council also recommended a federal review of human embryo research, preimplantation genetic diagnosis, and genetic modification of embryos and gametes in order to develop public policies for the field (President's Council on Bioethics 2002: ch. 8). To date there is no federal legislation in the United States prohibiting reproductive cloning.

In 1997, the Council of Europe adopted the Convention for the Protection of Human Rights and Dignity of the Human Being with Regard to the Application of Biology and Medicine. The Convention aims at the protection of human dignity which may be undermined by biomedical developments and has been signed by 34 countries and ratified by 21. Article 1 of the Convention requires parties to the Convention to '...protect the dignity and identity of all human beings and guarantee everyone, without discrimination, respect for their integrity and other rights and fundamental freedoms with regard to the application of biology and medicine'.

The Convention does not specifically proscribe human cloning, raising interesting questions about whether cloning was covered by the provisions of the Convention relating to dignity (Bell 1999: 220–21). In 1998, the Council of Europe adopted an Additional Protocol to the Convention for the Protection of Human Rights and Dignity of the Human Being with Regard to the Application of Biology and Medicine, on the Prohibition of Cloning Human Beings. The adoption of this Additional Protocol clarified the proscription of cloning for those members of the Council of Europe who signed the Additional Protocol (ibid.: 221). The Protocol has been signed by 31 countries and ratified by 16. Part of the Preamble to the

Protocol notes that 'the instrumentalisation of human beings through the deliberate creation of genetically identical human beings is contrary to human dignity and thus constitutes a misuse of biology and medicine.' Article 1 of the Protocol prohibits 'Any intervention seeking to create a human being genetically identical to another human being, whether living or dead'.

The United Nations Economic, Scientific and Cultural Organisation (UNESCO) approved a Universal Declaration on the Human Genome and Human Rights in 1997. Article 1 of the Declaration highlights the value of diversity: 'The human genome underlies the fundamental unity of all members of the human family, as well as the recognition of their inherent dignity and diversity. In a symbolic sense, it is the heritage of humanity.'

Article 2 of the Declaration states:

a) Everyone has a right to respect for their dignity and for their rights regardless of their genetic characteristics.
b) That dignity makes it imperative not to reduce individuals to their genetic characteristics and to respect their uniqueness and diversity.

The Declaration also opposes cloning stating: 'practices which are contrary to human dignity, such as reproductive cloning of human beings, shall not be permitted' (Article 11).

Even in the area of reproductive cloning, the articulation of common values at an international level has been fraught with difficulties (Annas, Andrews and Isasi 2002; Shanin 2002). In 2005, the General Assembly of the United Nations approved the United Nations Declaration on Human Cloning which *inter alia* called upon Member States 'to prohibit all forms of human cloning inasmuch as they are incompatible with human dignity and the protection of human life' (Declaration, para. b). The resolution to adopt the Declaration was passed by a vote of 84–34 with 37 abstentions. The UN Declaration may have little practical effect. Its non-binding nature means individual countries will be able to develop their own interpretation of the provisions.

The concept of human dignity is clearly an ever-present feature of debates over human cloning and, within bioethics more generally. Indeed, the language of human dignity is utilized with increasing frequency in debates about biomedical advances. Calls for a 'dignitarian' approach to science are informed by a range of different perspectives, including communitarian and religious views, and together form what Roger Brownsword has called a 'dignitarian alliance' which is bound together by a shared concern for the protection of human dignity (Brownsword 2004a: 20). As Brownsword points out, appeals to dignitarianism present regulators and policy-makers with major challenges insofar as they reject regulatory options based on appeals to pluralism and compromise. After all, if one believes that research on human embryos is intrinsically wrong and a threat to human dignity, then proposals for regulatory frameworks which impose strict requirements on, but none the less permit, embryo research are unlikely to be regarded as satisfactory solutions (2004a: 26–7).

Implicit within the claims that cloning is an affront to human dignity is the idea that it is cloning *per se* that is harmful (Pattinson 2002: 306). However, Shaun Pattinson has argued that 'for one's rights to be violated, one must have been denied of an alternative existence wherein one's rights are fulfilled'. Pattinson argues:

> The use of a cloning technique appears to be a necessary condition for the existence of any particular cloned individual and, even if it were not, there is no reason to assume that any alternative existence would be any better for that individual. Therefore, unless one makes a number of highly implausible and unprovable metaphysical assumptions, a cloned individual's right cannot have been violated by its mere cloning. [2002: 305]

Others have also questioned whether cloning is wrong *per se*. In sharp contrast to the calls to ban cloning as a threat to human dignity and the integrity of the species, some commentators have argued that, if concerns over safety can be overcome, cloning presents society with other possibilities, including an alternative expression of reproductive freedom, a solution to the ageing of the population, and an important aspect of research in a technologically advanced society (Lee 2004).

So what is this thing called 'human dignity' and is it threatened by the possibilities inherent in our future technologies? Richard Ashcroft has argued that there are currently four distinct scholarly groups in debates over dignity. The first group is that of the 'dignity sceptics', who are not convinced that dignity is a useful concept, and who comprise, in Ashcroft's view 'the mainstream of current English[-]speaking bioethics' (2005: 679). The second group finds dignity a useful concept in some ways, 'but strictly reducible to autonomy as extended to cover some marginal cases' (ibid.: 679). For the third group, dignity is part of a 'family of concepts about capabilities, functionings, and social interactions' while the final group regards dignity 'as a metaphysical property possessed by all and only human beings' (ibid.: 679). While an analysis of these different groups is beyond the scope of this chapter, Ashcroft's analysis does serve to remind us that the concept of dignity itself is contested. Certainly the concept of dignity is central to contemporary cloning debates. It has been described 'as the conceptual keystone in international instruments dealing specifically with biomedicine and genetics' (Bell 1999: 219). Yet, as Bell points out, 'for such a central concept in international human rights law, there has been virtually no commentary on human dignity – its source, content or boundaries' (ibid.). Timothy Caulfield and Roger Brownsword have argued that the concept of dignity, as it is used in bioethical debates, needs to be clarified further: 'for [dignity] to be a legitimate, useful policy tool, regulators need to be clear about how and why human dignity is implicated. Without such clarity, the concept of human dignity is in danger of devolving into a hollow rhetorical slogan' (Caulfield and Brownsword 2006: 76).

Defining the Clone

Prior to 2002, when the Federal Parliament enacted the Prohibition of Human Cloning Act, there was limited Australian legislation regulating cloning. That legislation which did exist was at a state level and only existed in those states – Victoria, South Australia and Western Australia – that had legislation regulating reproductive technologies. Each of these states had statutory provisions that specifically banned human cloning as part of their regulation of reproductive technologies. However, these three states had different definitions of cloning. In Victoria, section 3 of the Infertility Treatment Act 1995 defined 'clone' as 'to form, outside the human body, a human embryo that is genetically identical to another human embryo or person'. In South Australia, the Reproductive Technology Code of Ethical Clinical Practice, which is contained in a schedule to the Reproductive Technology (Code of Ethical Clinical Practice) Regulations 1995, defined 'cloning' in clause 1 as 'any procedure directed at producing two or more genetically identical embryos from the division of one embryo'. In Western Australia, 'cloning' was defined in section 3 of the Human Reproductive Technology Act 1991 as 'the use of reproductive technology for the purpose of producing, from one original, a duplicate or descendant that is, or descendants that are, genetically identical, live born and viable'. As discussed below, in 2000 federal legislation prohibiting cloning was introduced with the Gene Technology Act 2000 (Cth) and since 2002, the area has been regulated by comprehensive federal legislation with mirror state legislation.

In other states and territories, guidelines issued by the National Health and Medical Research Council (NHMRC) provided ethical guidance on the clinical practice and research in reproductive technologies. The *Ethical Guidelines on Assisted Reproductive Technology* published by the NHMRC in 1996 listed a number of practices which are 'ethically unacceptable and should be prohibited' including: 'Experimentation with the intent to produce two or more genetically identical individuals, including development of human embryonal stem cell lines with the aim of producing a clone of individuals' (1996: para. 11.3). The NHMRC *Guidelines* also imposed limitations on embryo research. These guidelines were superseded by new guidelines issued by the NHMRC in 2004 and updated in 2007.

The enactment of the Gene Technology Act 2000 (Cth) provided a prohibition of cloning within federal legislation, although given the constitutional limits on the powers of the federal government, the provision had only limited coverage. Section 192B of the Act prohibited cloning of human beings and defined 'cloning of a whole human being' as 'the use of technology for the purpose of producing, from one original, a duplicate or descendant that is, or duplicates or descendants that are, genetically identical to the original'.

In August 1999, the House of Representatives Standing Committee on Legal and Constitutional Affairs was given a reference by the Federal Minister for Health to inquire into the scientific, ethical and regulatory aspects of human cloning. In its report in 2001, the Committee noted the problems associated with the existing legislative definitions of cloning which focused on the clone being genetically identical to the original (House of Representatives, Standing Committee on Legal and Constitutional Affairs 2001: para. 8.33). The Committee noted that with somatic cell nuclear transfer, the mitochondrial DNA from the denucleated cell will form part of the DNA of the offspring, meaning that there could be slight differences between the offspring and the original donor. The Committee noted that

> ...the existing legislative definitions of the term 'cloning' focus on the final product of the process (that is an embryo or a person) being identical. On the other hand, scientific explanations appear to focus on the process itself not the final product. [ibid.: para. 8.36]

The Committee recommended the enactment of Commonwealth legislation to regulate human cloning and stem cell research and recommended that the legislation cover both public and privately funded research in these areas (ibid.: recommendations 1 and 2). The Committee recommended that the proposed legislation be separate from legislation regulating reproductive technologies (ibid.: para. 12.29), since the development of future research in this area 'will involve large biotechnology interests and major research projects. The products of this research could potentially be applicable in broad areas of clinical and medical practice that go a long way beyond reproductive technologies' (ibid.: para. 12.31). Under the proposed legislation, research involving the use of cloning technologies or using human embryos would be subject to a national licensing scheme, with the Committee recommending that the legislation contain a ban on human cloning for reproductive purposes (ibid.: recommendations 4–7).

Following the recommendations of the Report, Australia enacted federal legislation to prohibit human cloning[2] and regulate the use of cloning techniques in research.[3] The Prohibition of Human Cloning Act 2002 defined a 'human embryo clone' in section 8 as 'a human embryo that is a genetic copy of another living or dead human, but does not include a human embryo created by the fertilisation of a human egg by human sperm'.

For the purposes of the legislation, it is not necessary for the clone to be an identical genetic copy in order for it to be a genetic copy of another person (s. 8(2)). This definition of a 'human embryo clone' covers the creation of an embryo by a number of techniques, including: somatic cell nuclear transfer (SCNT) (the technique that produced Dolly the sheep), embryos formed by embryo splitting, nuclear transfer using non-somatic cells (such as embryonic stem cells), and parthenogenesis (Lockhart Review 2005: 55). The Act prohibited the following cloning practices:

- creating a human embryo clone (s. 9);
- intentionally placing a human embryo clone into the body of a person or animal (s. 10), and
- importing or exporting a human embryo clone into/from Australia (s. 11).

The Act also prohibited a number of other practices relating to use of gametes or embryos:

- creating a human embryo other than by fertilisation of a human egg with human sperm (s. 13);
- intentionally creating a human embryo outside a woman's body unless it is with the intention of attempting to achieve a pregnancy in the woman (s. 14);

---

2 Prohibition of Human Cloning Act 2002 (Cth).

3 Research Involving Human Embryos Act 2002 (Cth).

- creating or developing a human embryo with more than two genetic parents (s. 15);
- developing an embryo outside a woman's body for more than 14 days (s. 16);
- using precursor cells from an embryo or fetus to create an embryo (s. 17);
- altering the genome so that the alterations are heritable (s. 18);
- removing a viable embryo from a woman's body (s. 19);
- creating chimeras or hybrid embryos (s. 20);
- placing an animal embryo in a human, placing a human embryo in an animal, or placing an embryo in a human other than in a woman's reproductive tract (s. 21);
- importing or exporting prohibited embryos or placing an embryo into a woman's body and being reckless as to whether the embryo is a prohibited embryo (s. 22), and
- commercial trading in human gametes or embryos (s. 23).

The Research Involving Human Embryos Act 2002 (Cth) (hereafter RIHE Act) regulates the use of excess embryos from assisted reproductive technology (ART) programmes. An 'excess ART embryo' was defined in section 9 as one that had been created by ART for use in the ART treatment of a woman and that was excess to the needs of the woman and her spouse (if any) and where the woman and her spouse (if any) had determined that the embryo was excess to their needs and had given written authority for its use for a purpose other than the treatment of the woman.

The Act made it an offence for a person intentionally to use an excess ART embryo unless it is in accordance with a licence, or the use is exempt from the requirement for a licence under the provisions of the Act (s. 10). It is also an offence intentionally to use a human embryo that is not an excess ART embryo, if a person knows or is reckless of this fact, for a purpose that is not related to the treatment of a woman by an accredited ART centre (s. 11). The intentional or reckless breaching of a licence condition is also an offence (s. 12).

The RIHE Act established the Embryo Research Licensing Committee as a Principal Committee of the National Health and Medical Research Council (s. 13). The Committee has the power to make determinations on applications for licences for use of excess ART embryos. However, the Act originally restricted approval of uses that would damage or destroy an excess ART embryo to embryos created before 5 April 2002 (s. 21(3)(b)). The Act also required that an independent review of the Act be carried out as soon as possible after the second anniversary of the date on which the Act received Royal Assent (s. 47).

The Australian states also enacted mirror legislation to ensure the existence of a comprehensive legislative framework prohibiting cloning practices.[4] In 2004 the

4 Research Involving Human Embryos and Prohibition of Human Cloning for Reproduction Act 2003 (Qld); Human Cloning for Reproduction and Other Prohibited Practices Act 2003 (NSW); Research Involving Human Embryos (New South Wales) Act 2003 (NSW); Infertility Treatment Act 1995 (Vic); Prohibition of Human Cloning Act 2003 (SA); Research Involving Human Embryos Act 2003 (SA); Human Cloning and Other Prohibited Practices Act 2003 (Tas); Human Embryonic Research Regulation Act 2003 (Tas); Human Cloning and Embryo Research Act 2004 (ACT); Human Reproductive Technology Act 1991 (WA).

National Health and Medical Research Council issued *Ethical Guidelines on the Use of Assisted Reproductive Technology in Clinical Practice and Research* which referred to the federal legislation.

A review of the 2002 legislation, chaired by the Hon. John Lockhart AO, QC, recommended the continued prohibition of a number of practices including reproductive cloning (Lockhart Review 2005: 163), and implanting an embryo into a woman's body where the embryo is formed by means other than fertilization of an egg by sperm (ibid.: 165). The review also recommended that excess embryos from assisted reproductive technology should continue to be permitted for use in licensed research (ibid.: 167). The Committee also considered the use of somatic cell nuclear transfer to create human embryo clones from which embryonic stem cell lines could be developed and noted the different regulatory frameworks that exist in some other countries:

> The Committee heard that research using human cloning to generate embryonic stem cells is proceeding in several other countries where these technologies are legislatively permitted (e.g. United Kingdom, South Korea, Singapore) or where no national legislative regulations are in place (e.g. United States). Therefore, many respondents to the reviews argued that the prohibition of human cloning to generate patient-matched stem cells should be lifted in Australia to allow Australian researchers to continue to contribute to the intellectual and biotechnological developments in this field. [ibid.: 170]

The Committee recommended that the creation of embryos using somatic cell nuclear transfer should be permitted in Australia under licence (ibid.: 171; see also Cooper 2006).

The Prohibition of Human Cloning for Reproduction and the Regulation of Human Embryo Research Amendment Act 2006 (Cth) was enacted in 2006, taking effect from 12 June 2007. The Act changed the name of the Prohibition of Human Cloning Act 2002 to the Prohibition of Human Cloning for Reproduction Act 2002 and expanded the list of practices that were permitted with a licence. Following the amendments, the Prohibition of Human Cloning for Reproduction Act 2002 now permits the following activities to be carried out when authorised by a licence:

- creation of a human embryo other than by fertilisation, or the development of such an embryo (s. 22);
- creation or development of a human embryo which contains the genetic material from more than two persons (s. 23);
- creation or development of a human embryo using human embryonic or human fetal precursor cells (s. 23A);
- creation of a hybrid embryo (s. 23B).

It is an offence to carry out any of these activities without a licence. The Research Involving Human Embryos Act 2002 now permits the following practices when authorised by a licence:

- use of a human embryo that is created by a process other than fertilisation of a human egg by human sperm; using an embryo that has been created other than by fertilisation where the embryo contains genetic material from more than two persons; or use of a human embryo that was created using human embryonic or human fetal precursor cells (s. 10A);
- use of a hybrid embryo (s. 10A);
- research or training involving fertilisation of a human egg by human sperm, before the first mitotic division, outside a woman's body for the purposes of ART research or training (s. 10B).

It is an offence to carry out these activities without a licence. The Research Involving Human Embryos Act 2002 includes the requirement that the NHMRC Licensing Committee must not issue a licence unless it is satisfied that the proposed project has been assessed and approved by a Human Research Ethics Committee (HREC) that is constituted in accordance with the NHMRC's *National Statement on Ethical Conduct in Human Research* 2007 (RIHE Act s. 21(3)(c)). In 2007 the NHMRC's *Ethical Guidelines on the Use of Assisted Reproductive Technology in Clinical Practice and Research* were revised to take account of the amendments to the federal legislation (NHMRC 2007a).

In the United Kingdom, the Human Genetics Advisory Commission and the Human Fertilisation and Embryology Authority published *Cloning Issues in Reproduction, Science and Medicine* in 1998. This report suggested that the government consider legislation explicitly banning reproductive cloning (1998: para. 9.2). In addition, the report recommended that the Secretary of State for Health consider regulations covering two purposes for which the Human Fertilisation and Embryology Authority could issue licences: (i) 'developing methods of therapy for mitochondrial diseases', and (ii) 'developing methods of therapy for diseased or damaged tissues or organs' (ibid.: para. 9.3).

As in Australia, definitional issues have been of concern in the United Kingdom. The Human Fertilisation and Embryology Act 1990 requires a licence in order to create, keep or use an embryo (s. 3(1)). Section 3(3)(d) of the Act provides that 'A licence cannot authorise...(d) replacing a nucleus of a cell of an embryo with a nucleus taken from a cell of any person, embryo or subsequent development of an embryo.'

Since the technique used to create Dolly involved replacing the nucleus of an egg rather than an embryo, the scope and application of the Act to an embryo created by cell nuclear replacement techniques was uncertain (Lee and Morgan 2001b: 93; Pattinson 2002: 296). In 2002, the Court of Appeal held that cell nuclear replacement was covered by the 1990 Act,[5] although the government had passed the Human Reproductive Cloning Act 2001 in response to a decision by the High Court in 2001 holding that cell nuclear replacement was not covered by the Act.[6] The Human Reproductive Cloning Act 2001 prohibited placing an embryo in a woman's body if the embryo had been created other than by fertilization.

5 *R (on the application of Quintavalle) v. Secretary of State for Health* [2002] EWCA Civ 29.

6 *R (on the application of Quintavalle) v. Secretary of State for Health* [2001] EWHC Admin 918. For discussion of these UK developments, see Pattinson 2002: 296–7.

Genetics and Identity

What is so fascinating about the debate over cloning is that opposition to cloning is often articulated by an appeal to diversity. There is concern that the deliberate creation of a delayed twin through cloning represents an affront to the rights of the cloned individual by robbing them of their potential (or right?) to genetic uniqueness. So the appeal to diversity rests on a view that there is something ethically suspect about the deliberate creation of an individual who is the genetic twin of another person – that the deliberate creation of sameness is wrong.

As discussed above, since a large part of the unease over cloning rests on the deliberate creation of genetic sameness, opposition to cloning makes an appeal to diversity (Hartouni 1997: 119). The fascinating thing about this appeal is that it is so strikingly at odds with the general cultural push away from the particular and towards the universal. The appeal to diversity in the cloning debate stands in stark contrast to the way that diversity has been problematized in other areas. Contemporary debates over multiculturalism and over the rights of and obligations to indigenous communities, for example, are founded on a tension between recognition and respect for difference and the centripetal forces of the dominant culture. As Valerie Hartouni notes (ibid.: 119), 'even a casual glance across the cultural landscape suggests that far from being richly appreciated, embraced, or encouraged, diversity and difference are often addressed as discrepancy or deviance and, in either case, as problems to be managed.'

It is useful to contrast the way that diversity is utilized in the cloning debates with its use in broader debates over genetics. One of the goals in the mapping of the human genome is to gain a better understanding of the genetic basis of certain diseases or conditions. The ultimate goal is, of course, not simply the identification of these conditions but the development of treatments that would effect a cure. With the identification of certain conditions as genetic in origin we are not only finding a physical source for these conditions, we are also identifying certain conditions as departures from the 'normal'. As Evelyn Fox Keller points out, the quest for genetic health leads us to look for the bases for 'genetic unhealth'. We are seeking freedom from 'disease-causing genes' in the quest for normality yet, as Keller points out, we can only define normality by the absence of these problem genes (1992: 298).

In the debates over genetics then, there are two different threads that can be identified. On the one hand, we have debates about genetics and the identification of genetic disease which rely on an appeal to normality, even though the concept of normality itself remains rather elusive. These debates rest not on an appeal to diversity, but rather quite the opposite, for difference may be associated with a departure from genetic normality that is seen as undesirable. On the other hand, the debate over cloning rests on an appeal to diversity. In this sense, the cloning debate really seems quite remarkable when viewed against other debates over genetics. Yet if we look closely at it, we can see that the concerns over genetic sameness evident in the cloning debate are not really a celebration of difference and diversity. In fact, the concept of diversity as utilized in cloning debates really serves to reinforce sameness. It is, after all, the fact that we all have different DNA that makes us the same. Cloning would challenge that because in a clonal world, some people would have naturally generated, different DNA, while others would have DNA that duplicates that of another.

What is evident in the debate over cloning is the conflation of identity with genetics (Bell 1999). As Dreyfuss and Nelkin argue, 'Genetic essentialism posits that personal traits are predictable and permanent, determined at conception, "hard-wired" into the human constitution' (1992: 320–21). At its extreme forms, genetic essentialism would see people purely as the product of their genes. Even if the relevance of culture and environment in forming an individual is acknowledged, the appeal of the apparent certainty and neutrality of science is very strong. As Evelyn Fox Keller has pointed out, 40 years ago, biology and culture were clearly divided. Today however, 'the very notion of "culture" as distinct from "biology" seems to have vanished' (ibid.: 297). Just as in the broader debates over genetics we are all the products of our genes (at least to some degree), the cloned individual is also genetically determined, but even more so since his or her genes are already 'owned' by someone else. While we are all now seen as the products of our genes, the clone in particular seems to be characterized as an asocial creation. As Valerie Hartouni says:

> The individual of the cloning controversy emerges rather as a self-evident fact of nature or a fixed, stable, noncontingent value. It is an utterly nonrelational entity, indeed, an entity whose definitive features – whose individuality, authenticity, unique difference, or thoroughly contained and autonomous self – are regarded as genetically inscribed, guaranteed, and given properties, the potential theft or (unauthorized) appropriation of which may now require policing. [1997: 125]

Yet to the extent that concerns over cloning are founded on the perceived threat to individuality by the owning of DNA that is identical to another's, those concerns succumb to a view of humanity in which one's life story is written in DNA code, inscribed in our make-up in the same way that computer software comes preinstalled and defines the scope of the tasks that may be performed on that particular machine. The appeal of genetics is very strong. Yet in a world of genetic determinism, where is the space for the influence of culture and environment in forming an individual? Where is the space for individual agency, for our ability to write our own lives, or to install new 'software'?

Advances in genetic science undoubtedly hold the promise of a bold and exciting future. In 50 years' time, we may look back on this time as an age of discovery. But it is also possible that we look back and see a time of tragic social wrongs and inadequate legal safeguards. The task for lawyers and others is to ensure that the processes of legal reform are informed by social as well as scientific versions of the future. When we consider the story told by the new genetics, it is important to remember that what is written in code is only the introduction. The rest of the story we write ourselves.

Chapter 4

Reproductive Rights in a Posthuman World

For those of us who live in Western liberal democratic societies, free choice is something that we take for granted. We are able to choose where we live, who our friends are, where we work, and what our priorities are in life. Choice is, of course, never entirely without limits. Both the law and social morality limit the exercise of choices that may be harmful to others. Furthermore, our choices over where we work may be limited by the realities of the labour market and many of our choices and opportunities may be confined by socially constructed realities of class, gender, race and disability. Yet even while we acknowledge these limits, the rhetoric of choice and autonomy is a strong and central feature of contemporary society. Choice is, it seems, an inbuilt feature of our lives.

This chapter is about the role of law in regulating individual choice both now and into the future. In particular, it is about the regulatory choices we will be forced to make as we move into an age where parents may be able increasingly to choose the characteristics of their children. For some, these technological possibilities have the potential to propel us towards a bleak and impoverished future. For others it is a future full of sparkling possibilities. And in between is a rocky terrain of difficult choices and tough decisions.[1]

As society debates both the possibilities and limitations associated with advances in medical science, regulatory questions also emerge. What is the most appropriate form of regulation for scientific research and development? How do we best strike a balance between individual and community protection on the one hand, and the advancement of scientific knowledge on the other? How do we determine the content of laws designed to regulate modern medical science? If the law is intended to be a reflection of community values, how do we best determine the content of laws in areas in which community views differ widely? What particular challenges emerge as we seek to formulate regulatory solutions within federal systems? How are our regulatory options shaped by global regulatory trends and developments?

Genetic Transformations

It is in the area of reproduction that advances in medical science and technology seem set to have a profound effect. As we move into a future that is shaped by genetics, cloning technologies, assisted conception and advances in medicines, the

1 For further analysis of these themes, see Chapter 1.

possibility of shaping human characteristics is approaching reality. Prospective parents may be able to select embryos based on their characteristics. Already we can test embryos that are being used in assisted conception for genetic disorders using a technique called 'preimplantation genetic diagnosis' (PGD), giving us the ability to choose to implant only those embryos that are unaffected by genetic disease. Provided we can identify the particular genetic mutations associated with disease, we may also be able to identify and select against late-onset conditions that would only affect an individual in later life (Verlinsky et al. 2002). The same technique could be used for sex selection so that prospective parents could choose only to have embryos of a particular sex transferred to the woman's body. It is already possible to combine the use of PGD with tissue-matching technologies to ensure that we select an embryo that would develop into a child whose cord blood or other tissue would be compatible for an existing sick child in need of a transplant (Verlinsky et al. 2001; Verlinsky et al. 2004). The screening out of unhealthy embryos, and the creation of 'saviour siblings' (Spriggs and Savulescu 2002; Bennett 2005) shows that we are already making choices over the genetic and other characteristics of future individuals. To date, there has not been widespread use of preimplantation genetic diagnosis – with approximately one hundred babies born in the UK following PGD and approximately one thousand world-wide (Human Genetics Commission 2006: para. 4.1). At present, PGD is used for diagnosis of genetic disorders, for women who have previously terminated a pregnancy following prenatal screening or diagnosis, or for women who are at risk of passing on a genetic disorder but for whom termination of pregnancy is unacceptable (ibid.: para. 4.10).

The potential to select embryos on the basis of their characteristics raises concerns about the potential eugenic impact of the technologies. There are also concerns that parents may begin to select for other non-medical reasons, such as eye colour, intelligence, height, or athletic ability, if we were able to identify accurately the genes for these characteristics. Finally, there are also concerns that we may, in time, be able to manipulate human genetic make-up, paving the way for changes to the human germline that would be inherited by subsequent generations. Indeed, Francis Fukuyama has argued in his book *Our Posthuman Future* 'that the most significant threat posed by contemporary biotechnology is the possibility that it will alter human nature and thereby move us into a "posthuman" stage of history' (2002: 7). Futurist Ray Kurzweil has argued that humanity is moving towards what he calls 'the Singularity', that is, 'a future period during which the pace of technological change will be so rapid, its impact so deep, that human life will be irreversibly transformed' (2005: 7). There is a very real sense in which developments in genetic science and medical technology are taking us away from the genetic lottery of previous generations and towards a new future based on technology and choice. We are moving, to borrow from the title of a book by Allen Buchanan and others, 'from chance to choice' (Buchanan et al. 2000).

Let us imagine the story of a young couple, whom we can call Tony and Lucy. They live in the future, although a future that is not so very far from the present. They live in a major city in a wealthy Western country and have a nice house in the suburbs. Tony and Lucy would like to have a child. Both have previously undergone genetic testing, a precondition for their employment and for their life insurance.

They are aware that they both carry a gene for cystic fibrosis, a recessive genetic disorder that is common in people of northern European ancestry, giving them a one in four risk in each pregnancy of having a child affected by cystic fibrosis. Lucy's family also has a history of breast cancer. Given their genetic profiles, they decide that it is better not to risk the genetic lottery of natural conception and decide instead to conceive using assisted conception technologies. When Lucy's eggs are fertilized, the resulting embryos are tested, using preimplantation genetic diagnosis. Those embryos that carry the genes for cystic fibrosis or for breast cancer will not be used to conceive a child and are, with Tony and Lucy's consent, donated for medical research. Tony and Lucy meet with their doctor to discuss the use of the remaining embryos. They explain to their doctor that they would like their first-born child to be a boy and, since there are a number of tall, athletic people in Lucy's family, they would also like to select those embryos that have the genetic markers for both height and athletic ability. In making these choices, Tony and Lucy are motivated by a concern to give their child the best possible start in life and a belief that height and athletic ability will be valuable attributes as their future son grows up.

Disability and Choice

What are we to think about Tony and Lucy's decision? Is this simply an exercise of parental choice or is it a new form of eugenics? The development of preimplantation genetic diagnosis raises the ethical question of whether the technology is inherently eugenic. Similar issues arise in relation to the use of PGD for sex selection. Does the selective discarding of certain embryos represent a denigration of people with disabilities, or in the case of sex selection, of women? Is it wrong for prospective parents to choose to implant only those embryos that are not affected by particular genetic characteristics?

The idea of selecting embryos on the basis of their genetic characteristics or other characteristics sounds to many like a new form of eugenics. Popular in the late nineteenth and early twentieth century, eugenics was a theory that posited that the human race could be improved if the genetically 'fit' members of society reproduced and the genetically 'unfit' members of society were discouraged from reproducing (World Health Organisation 2002a: 162–3). Eugenic ideology led to the introduction of sterilization programmes in some countries and many women who were regarded as genetically inferior were sterilized. The combination of eugenic ideology and mass exterminations during the Nazi era led to the discrediting of eugenics and the theory fell from favour (ibid.: 162).

In the context of modern genetics, there is no suggestion of the reintroduction of state-enforced eugenic programmes aimed at improving the human gene pool. Indeed, some commentators have argued that there is no threat from genetic technologies as long as the decision-making power stays in the hands of individual parents and is not imposed by the state. In Britain, the House of Commons Science and Technology Committee's report, *Human Reproductive Technologies and the Law*, commented:

> If ensuring that your child is less likely to face a debilitating disease in the course of their life can be termed eugenics, we have no problem with its use. State programmes that impose a genetic blueprint are another matter. They should be outlawed as part of any regulation of assisted reproduction. Use of the word eugenics must not be used as an emotive term of abuse to obscure rational debate. [2005: para. 116]

With PGD, our decisions may be negative (selecting against an impairment), or they may be positive (selecting in favour of a particular feature) (Scott 2006: 163). As Rosamund Scott points out, 'In relation to all these kinds of selection, the helpful question is not which would be eugenic – since at one level they would all be – but how much we think it is appropriate to make these different kinds of selection decision' (ibid.).

Perhaps one of the most complex issues associated with the new genetics is to determine what reproductive autonomy means in the new context – to strike a balance between disability rights and reproductive rights. The ethics of abortion has always been complex. The ethics of abortion, and more recently of PGD, on the grounds of disability raises its own complexities for it raises the idea of selecting the traits of the offspring.

There is no doubt that the new genetics will impact on reproductive decision-making. In the short term, that impact is likely to be through an increased ability to diagnose genetic conditions that result in disability. However, with our increased focus on genetic health and an ability to diagnose an increasing number of conditions, we may be confronted with an increased range of information that will present ethical dilemmas for prospective parents and their medical advisers. We may, for example, be confronted with the results of genetic testing that identify pre-symptomatic and/or late-onset conditions, or that indicate that a child will be a carrier of a particular condition. How would such information be weighed by prospective parents in decision-making over whether to use such an embryo in ART or to continue such a pregnancy?

To a large degree, the debates over PGD resonate with those about termination of pregnancy following prenatal diagnosis of foetal disability (Jackson 2000; Scott 2005; Sheldon and Wilkinson 2001). The legal context obviously differs – the difference between the regulation imposed by abortion laws and the regulation imposed by reproductive technology laws. For some people, there would also be important moral differences between PGD, in which there is no pregnancy and no abortion of a developing foetus, and abortion which so clearly does involve terminating the life of a foetus (Botkin 1998: 20–21). However, since more embryos will be created than used, preimplantation genetic diagnosis may actually be seen by some as having greater ethical problems than abortion (ibid.: 21). What is clear is that the nature of reproductive autonomy and the significance of disability to reproductive decision-making are common territory for both PGD and prenatal diagnosis followed by abortion.

All prospective parents hope for a safe birth and a healthy child. It is understandable that prospective parents, when faced with a diagnosis of serious disability following preimplantation genetic diagnosis will be confronted with difficult choices. For couples who have chosen to use PGD to avoid having a child affected by a genetic condition, they may already be aware of the condition and may already have an affected child.

It is easy to see that the choices made by Tony and Lucy are not motivated by outdated eugenic theories but rather by a simple parental concern to make the best possible choices for their future child. But if decision-making is individualized does this mean that there is nothing to worry about? Might we come to regard couples who are undergoing *in vitro* fertilization and using PGD as having a moral duty to ensure that they have the best children possible, an obligation that Savulescu calls 'procreative beneficence'? Savulescu argues that 'Procreative Beneficence implies couples should employ genetic tests for non-disease traits in selecting which child to bring into existence and that we should allow selection for non-disease genes in some cases even if this maintains or increases social inequality' (2001: 415).

Concern has been expressed that the selecting-out of embryos on the basis of genetic make-up will have a detrimental impact on the interests of people with disabilities (Asch 1999). In choosing not to use certain embryos, are we reflecting broader negative social stereotypes of disability? Savulescu rejects this argument. He argues (ibid.: 423) that we need 'to distinguish between disability and persons with disability. Selection reduces the former, but is silent on the value of the latter.'

There is no doubt that the use of prenatal diagnosis and preimplantation genetic diagnosis will mean that some children who would have been born with disabilities will not in fact be born. It is also vitally important that parents receive good non-directive genetic counselling that assists them to make an informed decision. It is important to realize that, even if we use PGD, that it does not necessarily follow that the needs, rights and interests of individuals with disabilities are of lesser importance.[2] Disabilities occur for a wide variety of reasons and many disabilities are not genetic in origin. As Joan Rothschild has pointed out, 'Lost in the renewed obsession with genes and the precipitous rush to geneticize disability and disease is the critical fact that very few impairments have a genetic cause' (2005: 150). We only need to consider the extent of disability caused by accidents, and in particular, motor vehicle accidents, as well as the disability caused by illness and other medical conditions such as strokes, in order to realize that disability is likely to be part of the spectrum of the human condition for many years to come.

It may be that in time we will be able to treat many diseases and conditions that currently cause much illness and disability. In time, we may even be able to correct genetic disorders at the embryonic stage. Until such time, even if genetic screening technologies are used, we will still, as a society, need to ensure that our social and medical resources are adequate to meet the needs of those with disabilities as well as the needs of their carers and families, and that we have appropriate laws in place to provide protection against discrimination. Yet until we are able to treat or cure the genetic disorders that lead to disease and disability, it may not be realistic for us to expect that prospective parents will ignore factors that are relevant to the health of their future child when choosing which embryos to use. At the same time, however, we do need to be aware of the social context for the use of genetic screening

2 'Even in a world of widespread prenatal testing, society will still have to develop better ways of meeting the needs of many people with disabling conditions' (Green 1997: 12).

technologies. We do need to appreciate that the reproductive decisions that women and their partners make on a daily basis 'define the contours of the "imperfect child", as well as the "perfect child", socially, economically, and culturally' (Rothschild 2005: 9). As the President's Council on Bioethics in the United States pointed out:

> Although, at least in the United States, the practice of screening and elimination is likely to remain voluntary, its growing use could have subtly coercive consequences for prospective parents and could increase discrimination against the 'unfit.' Children born with defects that could have been diagnosed in utero may no longer be looked upon as 'Nature's mistakes' but as parental failings. [2003: 36–7]

There is still a great deal of work to be done in this area and it will be important for there to be ongoing dialogue between women's groups and the disability community, so that we can find ways of articulating shared interests in ways that are respectful of both reproductive rights and disability rights.

Sex Selection

The issue of sex selection also raises some profound issues for us. In the example of Tony and Lucy, they plan to use preimplantation genetic diagnosis to select not only against certain genetic conditions but also in order to select for embryos of a particular sex. Of course in some instances, sex selection is part of selecting against sex-linked inherited diseases. If a couple with a family history of haemophilia chooses not to use male embryos then they can eliminate the risk of having a child affected by the condition. This is because haemophilia is carried on the X chromosome which means that male children, who only have one copy of the X chromosome, are affected by the disease while female children, who have two copies of the X chromosome, may be carriers of the disease but will not be symptomatic.

In other instances though, sex selection may be sought for cultural rather than medical reasons. In many countries, there is a strong preference for male children. The reasons for this vary but include the potential for male children to grow into breadwinners, the financial burdens associated with the need to provide a dowry for a female child when she marries, and the socially and economically inferior position of girls and women in many societies. Even in societies where there is a greater degree of gender equality, there is often still a preference for the first-born child to be male.

Sex-selective technologies do have the potential to change the shape of society's demographics. It is possible that if large numbers of parents choose to have a male child either by selectively aborting female foetuses or by using PGD to select only male embryos, that there will be a disproportionate number of males born in the society. Sex selection raises complex issues about equity and reproductive choice in contemporary society (Danis 1995; McDougall 2005; Moazam 2004). In some Asian countries, including China and India, there are reports of high sex ratios at birth and in infancy. The sex ratio of a population is generally expressed in terms of the numbers of males per 100 females. More male babies are born but more male babies die during infancy, so although at birth the sex ratio may be as high as

106 males per 100 females, this tends to become more evenly balanced over time (Bannister 2004: 21; Wu, Viisainen and Hemminki 2006). However, in India there are reports of as few as 927 girls to 1000 boys in the 0–6 age group (Nidadavolu and Bracken 2006), and in China of 117 boys per 100 girls (Wu, Viisainen and Hemminki 2006; see also Bannister 2004). Several reasons have been given for these figures, including: (1) under-reporting of female births, (2) prenatal sex determination and selective abortion of female foetuses, and (3) high rates of female neonatal mortality (Bannister 2004; Wu, Viisainen and Hemminki 2006: 172). Despite laws in both India and China aimed at restricting or preventing the use of medical technology for sex-selective purposes, the enforcement of these laws has been difficult (Wu, Viisainen and Hemminki 2006: 178; Nidadavolu and Bracken 2006), posing practical challenges for the role of law in transforming community views.

Of course, in some countries parents may seek out sex-selective technologies for the purposes of 'family balancing', particularly where they already have one or more child of a particular sex. Some commentators have argued that sex selection may be morally tolerable in countries where there does not appear to be strong pro-male bias amongst prospective parents (Dickens 2002; Savulescu 1999). The American College of Obstetricians and Gynecologists' 2007 policy on sex selection supports sex selection for medical reasons, such as prevention of sex-linked genetic diseases, but opposes sex selection for personal reasons, including family balancing 'because of the concern that such requests may ultimately support sexist practices' (2007: 4). In Australia, the National Health and Medical Research Council guidelines on assisted reproductive technology state that 'pending further community discussion, sex selection (by whatever means) must not be undertaken except to reduce the risk of transmission of a serious genetic condition' (NHMRC 2007a: para. 11.1).

Choice and Parental Expectations

The idea that we may be able to select the traits of our children is, as John Robertson has argued, 'both appealing and disturbing' (1994: 150). We find the idea appealing because parents do want to have a healthy child (ibid.) but the idea also causes us to feel uneasy. As Robertson argues:

> The very concept of selection of offspring characteristics or 'quality control' reveals a major discomfort – the idea that children are objects or products chosen on the basis of their qualities, like products in a shop window, valued not for themselves but for the pleasure or satisfaction they will give parents. [ibid.]

The concern here is that the creation of children becomes an exercise of consumer choice rather than an acceptance of a child as a gift and a blessing. It may seem that we are playing God when we seek to have such a degree of control over our children.

Will parental expectations be shaped by the knowledge that they have chosen the characteristics of their children? What are the limits of parents' rights to choose in these circumstances? Would we, for example, feel comfortable allowing parents to select *for* a disability, such as deafness? (Häyry 2004). If we are able to select our children's characteristics, will we have even higher expectations of our children than we would if we had no control over their genetic make-up? If we consider the fictional case of Lucy and Tony that I discussed above, how will Lucy and Tony feel if they have chosen embryos with the genetic markers for height and athletic ability, but their son grows up as a very bookish kid who hates athletics and anything sporty? Of course, all parents have expectations, hopes and fears for their children. The question for us here is whether we will create additional, unrealistic expectations on the part of parents that might be damaging to children if we allow parents to choose their children's characteristics (Botkin 1998: 23).

Let us return to Tony and Lucy then. How do we evaluate the choices they have made? Some people may object to any use of preimplantation genetic diagnosis, on religious or other grounds. For others, some of the choices made by Tony and Lucy may be more acceptable than others. For example, is there an ethical difference between selecting for traits on the basis of medical grounds rather than non-medical reasons? These distinctions, if they can be made, may be significant in the crafting of regulatory frameworks for the use of these technologies.

Genetic Modification and Designer Babies?

So far, Lucy and Tony have been limited to using preimplantation genetic diagnosis to choose between their embryos on the basis of their existing characteristics. That is, they could choose not to use those embryos with the genetic markers for cystic fibrosis or breast cancer. They could choose to use only male embryos. They could also choose to select those embryos with genetic markers for height and athletic ability. But they could only choose between the available embryos that already had those characteristics – they could not change their characteristics. Let us move further into the future and imagine that Lucy and Tony are in fact able to ask their doctors to change the characteristics of their selected embryos. Although Tony and Lucy are both of only average height and are both pretty hopeless at sport, in the future world that they both inhabit their doctor may be able to manipulate the genetic make-up of the embryo actually to add in the desired characteristics.

Genetic manipulation may be either somatic gene therapy or germline gene therapy. Somatic gene therapy involves gene therapy of an individual and affects the somatic (non-reproductive) cells of the individual. If the therapy is successful, the changes will not be able to be passed on the individual's children because the reproductive cells remain unaffected by the therapy. Germline genetic therapy, on the other hand, would introduce changes to every cell in the patient's body, including the individual's germ cells (reproductive cells). The introduced changes would be inherited by subsequent generations (Association of Reproductive Health Professionals 2007: 5). Because of concerns over potential changes to the human germline, some countries, including Australia and Canada, have banned alterations to the human genome that could be inherited by subsequent generations.[3] Some commentators have argued that

3 See Prohibition of Human Cloning for Reproduction Act 2002 (Cth) (Australia) s. 15; Assisted Human Reproduction Act (2004) (Canada) para. 5(1)(f).

the threat posed by human cloning and inheritable genetic modification is so great that they should be regarded as 'crimes against humanity' (Annas, Andrews and Isasi 2002: 153). They argue that genetic modification technologies 'are techniques that can alter the essence of humanity itself (and thus threaten to change the foundations of human rights) by taking human evolution into our own hands and directing it towards the development of a new species' (ibid.).

The possibility of Tony and Lucy actively choosing genetic enhancement of their offspring is in the realm of the future. Our current knowledge of human genetics is far too limited for us to be able to manipulate the genome of individual embryos in meaningful ways. We simply do not have the knowledge to be able to manipulate the human genome so as to introduce desired enhancements. Many characteristics are multifactorial in nature, produced by interactions between genes or by a combination of both genetic and environmental factors. Even if we can identify the genes for intelligence, sexual orientation, or beauty, it is unlikely that any of these characteristics are purely genetic, thus complicating the task of genetic manipulation to actually introduce these features. As the President's Council on Bioethics commented in its report *Beyond Therapy*:

> In our considered judgment, these dreams of fully designed babies, based on directed genetic change, are for the foreseeable future pure fantasies. There are huge obstacles, both to accurate knowing and to effective doing. One of these obstacles – the reality that these traits are heavily influenced by environment – will not be overcome by better technology. [2003: 37–8]

Yet let us imagine for a moment though that we were able to perform reliable genetic enhancement. This conjures up an image of prospective parents choosing the characteristics of their children from a catalogue, in the same way as they might choose any other consumer item. The temptation to be able to improve ourselves, or at least to be able to improve our children, may be almost irresistible. Gregory Stock asks in his book *Redesigning Humans*, 'If you could safely add a genetic module to an embryo and thereby give your future child extra decades of healthy life, would you?' (2002: 78). Think of the appeal that these technologies would have. As Stock points out, 'The large markets for face-lifts, hair transplants, and Viagra are testimony to the difficulty of accepting the steady erosion of our vitality and youth' (ibid.: 79). We live in a world that is characterized, at least for the inhabitants of the wealthy countries of the world, by a condition that has been described as 'affluenza' – where it is never possible to have too much (Hamilton and Denniss 2005). In such a society, it seems unlikely that many would be able to resist the latest consumer product: the ability to modify one's offspring. Furthermore, in an increasingly competitive society, the desire by parents to give their child an extra advantage over others may be difficult to resist.

The use of genetic enhancement technologies by parents may also lead to what Francis Fukuyama and John Robertson have called a parental 'arms race', in which parents feel that they must use enhancement technologies for their children because other parents are doing so (Fukuyama 2002: 97; Robertson 2003: 479). Of course, one of the problems with such a race to enhancement is that, at least in the longer term, the benefits fade at the individual level. After all, if you decide to enhance your child's intelligence and athletic ability genetically, what have you gained if everyone else's child is also genetically enhanced for intelligence and athletic ability? Since enhancement is a relative concept, the greater the acceptance and use of enhancement technologies, the less advantage there is to those who actually use them and the greater the burden on those who do not participate (Fukuyama 2002: 97; Robertson 2003: 479).

The possibility of genetic enhancement raises the spectre of superhumans who have been genetically enhanced so as to provide them with additional advantages in life. There are fears that genetic enhancement technologies could lead to the development of a 'genetic overclass' (Fukuyama 2002: 157) that will increase social disparities. In a world of genetic enhancement, 'social elites may not just pass on social advantages but embed them genetically as well' (ibid.). There is a fear that the use of genetic enhancement could increase the gap between the haves and the have-nots (for discussion, see Shapiro 2002). This gap would be particularly acute at a global level since it is unlikely that the majority of people living in the developing countries of the world would be able to afford genetic enhancement technologies (Greenfield 2003: 143; World Health Organisation 2002a: 169). Might we ultimately have, as Susan Greenfield has suggested, 'a speciation, a divergence of the human race into two separate species, the "enhanced" and the "naturals"?' (2003: 143). And what would such differentiation mean for our traditional understandings of equality? James Watson, one of the co-discoverers of the structure of DNA, acknowledges that 'much of the public paranoia surrounding the dangers of human genetic manipulation is inspired by a legitimate recognition of our selfish side' (2004: 422). Yet Watson argues that 'ours is a uniquely social species' (ibid.: 423). For Watson, the evolutionary advantages associated with social cooperation mean that 'natural selection itself has likely endowed each of us with a desire to see others (and therefore our society) do well rather than fail' (ibid.).

We will need to work out whether the new genetic technologies should be available to all. If enhancement technologies become widely accepted in the future, we will need to consider what measures we will need to put in place to ensure that these technologies are not simply the preserve of the wealthy. Kurzweil argues that as technologies develop, they will also become less expensive and so more widely available:

> Each example of information technology starts out with early-adoption versions that do not work very well and that are unaffordable except by the elite. Subsequently the technology works a bit better and becomes merely expensive. Then it works quite well and becomes inexpensive. Finally it works extremely well and is almost free. The cell phone, for example, is somewhere between these last two stages. [2005: 469]

Yet if we seek to make enhancement technologies available to all, will this simply be a new form of state-sanctioned eugenics? Furthermore, we may simply be trading one form of inequality for another. As the President's Council on Bioethics pointed out in the context of equality of access to preimplantation genetic diagnosis: 'The worry over unequal access to PGD is, in effect, a worry about the inability of the *economically* poor to practice the ultimate discrimination against the *genetically* poor'

(2003: 52). One possibility is to aim to prohibit all forms of genetic enhancement, although even if we do prohibit the use of genetic enhancement, it seems unlikely that the issue will vanish entirely. Even with the prohibition of reproductive cloning in many national laws and in international declarations, the issue of cloning remains controversial, particularly at a global level.

The Erosion of Human Dignity?

Concerns about stem cell technologies and cloning are often expressed in terms of their threat to human dignity and the erosion of fundamental values (Brownsword 2003). The move towards posthumanism is often regarded as a constituting a threat to human dignity in ways that resonate with debates over dignity and human cloning. The Council of Europe's Convention on Human Rights and Biomedicine has as its stated purpose to 'protect the dignity and identity of all human beings and guarantee everyone, without discrimination, respect for their integrity and other rights and fundamental freedoms with regard to the application of biology and medicine' (Article 1). The Convention also prohibits genetic discrimination (Article 11), and rules out germline genetic modification: 'An intervention seeking to modify the human genome may only be undertaken for preventive, diagnostic or therapeutic purposes and only if its aim is not to introduce any modification in the genome of any descendants' (Article 13). Assisted conception technologies must not be used for sex selection 'except where serious hereditary sex-related disease is to be avoided' (Article 14).

In October 2005, UNESCO adopted a Universal Declaration on Bioethics and Human Rights. Article 3 of the Declaration states:

1. Human dignity, human rights and fundamental freedoms are to be fully respected.
2. The interests and welfare of the individual should have priority over the sole interest of science or society.

Article 11 states the principles of non-discrimination and non-stigmatization: 'No individual or group should be discriminated against or stigmatized on any grounds, in violation of human dignity, human rights and fundamental freedoms.' Article 16 has relevance for germline genetic modification. It states that 'The impact of life sciences on future generations, including in their genetic constitution, should be given due regard.'

In its report, *Human Cloning and Human Dignity*, the President's Council on Bioethics in the United States considered the use of enhancement technologies with human reproductive cloning. These technologies, the Council argued, would not aim to improve the health of sick individuals. Rather the aim would be to improve humanity:

> The effort may be guided by apparently good intentions: to improve the next generation and to enhance the quality of life of our descendants. But in the process of altering human nature, we would be abandoning the standard by which to judge the goodness or wisdom of the particular aims. We would stand to lose the sense of what is and is not human. [2002: 109]

The fear remains that in making these choices we may be changing the very essence of what it is to be human and that we may in the process be impoverishing ourselves both individually and communally. As we contemplate these technologies, we need to ask ourselves whether biotechnology really does place in our hands the power to reshape the very essence of what it means to be human. Do these developments put us teetering at the top of a slippery slope at the bottom of which is a high-tech yet impoverished future akin to Aldous Huxley's *Brave New World*?

Central to these concerns is a belief that we can discern the essence of what it is to be human and that it is this human essence that is threatened by the slide towards posthumanism. There should be little that is controversial in the claim that all human beings share features that entitle them to respect. Our contemporary concepts of equality and universal human rights are premised on understandings of commonality. Article 1 of the Universal Declaration of Human Rights states that 'All human beings are born free and equal in dignity and rights.' We can see a more genetically-focused declaration of equality and commonality in the UNESCO Declaration on the Human Genome and Human Rights, which states that 'The human genome underlies the fundamental unity of all members of the human family, as well as the recognition of their inherent dignity and diversity. In a symbolic sense, it is the heritage of humanity' (Article 1).

Drawing the dividing line between human and posthuman is not an easy task. Kurzweil asks:

> If we regard a human modified with technology as no longer human, where would we draw the defining line? Is a human with a bionic heart still human? How about someone with a neurological implant? What about two neurological implants? How about someone with ten nanobots in his brain? How about 500 million nanobots? Should we establish a boundary at 650 million nanobots: under that, you're still human and over that, you're posthuman? [2005: 374]

So could a posthuman individual have dignity, or are posthumanism and human dignity incompatible concepts? For those who believe that human dignity is undermined by moves towards posthumanism the two concepts are clearly incompatible. Others, however, have argued that it is possible to develop an understanding of posthuman dignity. Nick Bostrom has argued that we already live lives that are very different from those of our ancestors and that in the eyes of those ancestors 'we might already appear "posthuman"' (2005: 213). Bostrom argues that we have not been dehumanized by our current extensions of human abilities, life expectancies and knowledge, and that 'should we or our descendants one day succeed in becoming what relative to current standards we may refer to as posthuman, this need not entail a loss of dignity either' (ibid.).

One of the difficulties with the debates around dignity and genetics is that they seem to be entwined with a rather essentialistic view of the human genome. Dreyfuss and Nelkin have defined genetic essentialism as an approach that 'posits that personal traits are predictable and permanent, determined at conception, "hard-wired" into the human constitution' (1992: 320–21). Within conceptualizations of dignity that link human dignity to the immutability of the genome we can see the idea of essential human characteristics, encoded onto the human genome, that transcend time and culture and that might be at risk from genetic modification technologies. The idea that there are essential, immutable human characteristics has been challenged by scholars from postmodernism, feminism and critical race theory. Our understandings of the self and of the body have been cut free of their traditional anchors and have moved into a new arena where meanings are socially, culturally and historically constructed. While there is no doubt that in biological terms the genome itself has changed little in recent history, the same cannot be said of the genome's social and cultural significance. Increasingly, the genome has become the story of our identity, so that today it stands as a shorthand not only for who we are but also for why we are the way we are. As identity has been increasingly 'geneticized', so the significance of the genome has also changed and will continue to change (Karpin 2000). It is this cultural writing of the genome that will be so significant a part of the quest to retain human dignity, for it is not the biological information itself that may change human society but rather what we choose to do with that information. It is in relation to these choices that the law will play a vital role.

Conclusion: Enduring Values

The move towards the technological future confronts us with several possible visions that range from the bleakly technological society of *Brave New World* through to more positive visions of a society free of many of the diseases and conditions that shape contemporary society. It is impossible to foresee with any real accuracy which of these visions will ultimately prove to be closest to the truth – there are, after all, many forks in the road where choices which determine future direction will need to be made. We can, however, set out the values we will use to inform our choices and our law-making when we reach those forks in the road. Those values are equality and non-discrimination, respect for human rights, and justice.

Whatever path we take to the future it is imperative that our laws enshrine the principle of equality and provide protection from genetic discrimination. The politics of difference has had a rather ugly history through the ages and we must never forget the lessons of history lest we repeat the mistakes of the past. Respect for universal human rights extends these principles to a global level and requires that all persons be treated with dignity and respect, regardless of their genetic make-up and regardless of where they live. Principles of justice demand that we extend the benefits of technological advances to all people, being mindful that we do so in ways that do not compromise human rights.

It is too soon to say whether we will ultimately move to a world of genetic enhancement but our future has already been rewritten by genetic science. Already there are new stories and new possibilities for us. But there are a variety of different endings. It is up to us to make sure that those endings are ones that reflect the values of equality, human rights and justice.

Chapter 5

Health Rights and Health Tourism

The twentieth century was a time of huge advances in global wealth. Yet the distribution of this wealth has been very uneven and huge numbers of the world's population continue to live in conditions of dire poverty.[1] The transformations taking place within the global economy seem set to increase these gaps even further. Increasingly, the global economy seems to fracture along lines that constitute different rights and entitlements between the developed and developing worlds. In the developing world, debates over health are often debates over entitlements to the basic conditions for health, while in the developed nations, and particularly in the West, debates over health are increasingly individualized and articulated as rights claims to access high-tech and expensive health care. For the inhabitants of the developed world, modern health care has been transformed by the ease of travel and by affluent living conditions. Health consumers are increasingly both willing and able to travel in order to access the health services they require or desire. The global accessibility of commercialized health services raises important regulatory questions for the crafting of laws and policies at the national and international levels. Does international health tourism pose a challenge to the laws and policies of individual countries seeking to regulate health services within their borders? Should countries seek to restrict or limit health tourism? This chapter explores the development of health rights at a global level, analysing these issues at the interface between health and rights that exists in relation to the global movement of people and the development of health tourism as a global phenomenon.

Health Rights in a Global World

The developing world still bears a disproportionate impact in terms of the global burden of disease, including infectious disease. In 2001, there were 14.7 million deaths caused by infectious diseases – 26 per cent of total global mortality. Many of these deaths could have been prevented by currently available medicines and vaccines. Almost two million more could have been prevented by access to food and clean water (Kindhauser 2003: 6). While the mortality figures associated with infectious disease reveal the impact of disease on human society, they only tell part of the story. Across a whole range of indicators, including infant and maternal mortality rates (World Health Organisation 2004: Annex 7), the burden of disease and mortality

---

1 The gaps between wealth and extreme poverty have been growing. In 1900, the richest 20 per cent of the world's population had an income that was nine times that of the poorest 20 per cent. By 1997, the gap had grown so that the income of the richest 20 per cent was 70 times that of the poorest 20 per cent (Benatar, Daar and Singer 2003: 112–13).

is highest in the world's poorest countries. Three diseases alone – AIDS, TB and malaria – accounted for 5.6 million deaths in 2001, 39 per cent of all deaths from infectious disease (Kindhauser 2003: 6). These diseases impact disproportionately on the developing world. In 2003, only 11 per cent of the world's population lived in Africa, yet Africa was home to two-thirds of the world's people living with HIV/AIDS. Asia is home to one-fifth of the world's people living with HIV/AIDS (World Health Organisation 2004: 1). While the life expectancy in developed countries such as Australia is around 80 years, in some countries in the developing world it is around half that (ibid.: Annex 1). In sub-Saharan Africa, the impact of HIV/AIDS has reversed previous gains in life expectancy. In 2002, life expectancy at birth in the African Region was 48 years; without HIV/AIDS it would have been 54 (ibid.: 6). An estimated 14 million of the world's children, mainly living in Africa, have lost one or both parents to HIV/AIDS and it is estimated that by 2010 'anywhere from 15 per cent to 25 per cent of the children in a dozen sub-Saharan countries will be orphans' (ibid.: 8).

While the burden of disease has clear international demarcation lines based on the wealth of countries, there are also uneven distribution patterns in the benefits of advances in technology and medicines. Although developments in computers and telecommunications have transformed life in the developed world, their impact on life in developing countries is far more sporadic. The use of anti-retroviral treatments for HIV/AIDS is also very uneven (ibid.: 7), sparking debate about international patent laws and access to essential medicines. In genomics too, there is a need to address the growing gap in the distribution of benefits from biotechnological research (Dowdeswell, Daar and Singer 2003). In a World Health Organisation report, *Genomics and World Health*, it was noted that:

> A key concern is that the majority of the developing countries do not at present possess either the technological capacity or skill base to reap the potential benefits of genomics research and apply them to their health care needs. Furthermore, many countries have yet to establish the regulatory, ethical and policy frameworks that are required to address the economic, legal and social implications of this field, and safeguard against the potential risks and hazards of these technologies in the best interests of their populations. [2002a: 187–8]

Against the backdrop of these issues, the debate over whether there is a right to health, and debates over health rights generally, have taken on a new significance. In the developed nations of the world, the basic conditions for health (clean water, adequate sanitation, reasonable levels of public expenditure on health care, effective public health infrastructures, and so on) are all largely taken for granted. Concerns over health rights are instead articulated in ways that revolve around the availability and cost of access to the high-tech and expensive ends of health care. In Western countries, the landscape of health and health care has been transformed by the growing recognition of patients' rights and the drive towards consumerism (Darvall 1993). No longer is health care populated by patients and doctors. Today's health care is populated instead by health consumers and health service providers. This new landscape reshapes health and health rights in important ways that bring to the fore the economic dimensions of health and health care, transforming health care into an agreement over the provision of goods and services.

Although health rights are constructed and articulated in different ways in the developing and developed worlds, given the globalized nature of contemporary economies it should hardly be surprising that the health rights of different populations and economies of the world will intersect and overlap. Increasingly, these points of intersection are the subject of discussion and debate in the academic literature and by international bodies and agencies. They intersect over issues such as the disproportionate profile of biomedical research – the so-called '90/10 gap' where 90 per cent of the world's health research is directed towards 10 per cent of the world's population (Resnik 2004), over patent laws, benefit sharing and access to essential medicines (Brock 2001; Resnik 2001; UNESCO 2002), and over the development of academic disciplines such as bioethics where there has been increasing debate in recent years over the 'globalization of bioethics'. Health rights also coalesce around health tourism where the wealth of the inhabitants of the developed world meets the economic aspirations and vulnerabilities of the inhabitants and social and regulatory infrastructure of less wealthy countries. It is to this final point that the remainder of this chapter will be focused.

The Global Movement of People

Health rights and health tourism intersect around the movement of people across borders. This section will consider the intersection of those issues in four areas: (1) the international movement of health-care personnel, both for clinical care and for research; (2) the international movement of disease, a phenomenon that is driven by international trade and travel, including tourism; (3) procreative or fertility tourism, and (4) organ trafficking and 'transplant tourism'. This is not intended as an exhaustive list, for health tourism occurs in a variety of contexts, but rather the list here provides a few 'snapshots' of some of the areas in which health tourism can arise.

Health-care personnel

The disparities in health between countries outlined above are also reflected in the availability of health resources within countries. While the United States devoted 13.7 per cent of its GNP to health in 2001, in poorer countries the percentage of GNP devoted to health and annual per capita health expenditure is much smaller: 5.9 per cent of GNP in 2001 in Uganda, 1.6 per cent of GNP in Azerbaijan, and 2.6 per cent of GNP in 2001 in Somalia (World Health Organisation 2004: Annex 5).

The recruitment of developing-world health professionals by wealthy countries threatens the viability of the public health system of poor countries by reducing the small population of skilled professionals available for local populations. Although the Americas, including Canada and the United States, have only 10 per cent of the global burden of disease, this region spends more than 50 per cent of the global health-related financial resources and has nearly 37 per cent of the world's health-care workers (World Health Organisation 2006: 8). Africa has only three per cent of the world's health-care workers and less than one per cent of global health-related financial resources, despite having more than 24 per cent of the global burden of disease (ibid.: 8). The World Health Organisation has estimated that 57 of the world's poorest countries (36 of them in Africa) have a deficit of 2.4 million doctors, nurses and midwives (ibid.: 143).

Health professionals have long moved from poorer to richer countries to take advantage of better salaries and living conditions and improved educational and vocational opportunities. While migration of skilled professionals may lack the short-term qualities usually associated with tourism, such international movement of people is included here because of the link between health, health rights and the global movement of people.

The lack of access to trained health professionals is exacerbated by the migration of health professionals from rural to urban areas[2] and from poor countries to wealthy ones. This migration is driven by a range of factors including poor salaries for health professionals in developing countries and recruitment of health professionals by wealthy countries which face an increasing demand for skilled health professionals that they are unable to meet locally (Martineau, Decker and Bundred 2004; Scott et al. 2004). The migration of skilled health professionals from poor to rich countries is not neutral and the costs and benefits are unevenly distributed between developing and developed countries (Ahmad 2005: 43). For the developed countries, skilled migration means that they are able to save on educational costs, improve their global competitive position, gain increased capacity for innovation, and relieve short-term labour shortages. There are also benefits for developing countries, including remittances being sent home by workers and gains if skilled workers return home (ibid.). However, it has been argued that these benefits 'are trivial compared with the losses, which include loss of public educational investment, loss of intellectual capital, reduced range of available services, chronic understaffing of health facilities, and poor healthcare services' (ibid.).

The international movement of health professionals has been likened to a carousel, as health professionals move from one country to another and each country in turn then recruits internationally to fill its posts (Martineau, Decker and Bundred 2004: 3). Some countries, particularly in the developing world, are net exporters of personnel, some – mainly developed countries – are net importers and others are both exporters and importers (ibid.: 2). It has been argued that solving the 'brain drain' problem will require 'identification of key responsibilities of each main stakeholder group' with source countries addressing issues of staff retention and development assistance, and recipient countries focusing on ensuring that they are not permanently in need of health professionals from the South (ibid.: 9; Johnson 2005).

Health researchers may also migrate from one jurisdiction to another to avail themselves of research opportunities that are not available in their home jurisdiction – a phenomenon that has been described as 'research tourism' (Halliday 2004: 41). As Michael Kirby has noted, 'Faced with local legal prohibition, scientists may simply move their laboratories to countries with less restrictive laws' (2003: 16). In the context of research involving human subjects, there have been some attempts to formulate universal ethical principles that will apply to all researchers, wherever

2 For analysis of movement of health workers in Ethiopia, see Serneels et al. 2005.

they are located. In the period following the Second World War, the Nuremberg Code was developed as a guide for the ethical conduct of research involving human subjects. In 1964, the Declaration of Helsinki was published by the World Medical Association. This Declaration, which has been revised a number of times since the 1960s, is now widely regarded as the leading international declaration on the conduct of health-care research.[3] Yet even in the context of widely accepted international ethical guidelines, there has still been extensive debate over the significance of local cultural and economic specificities. In particular, debate has arisen over issues such as the cultural context for informed consent and the meaning of standards of care that may arise at the interface of the developing and the developed worlds when researchers from wealthy countries undertake healthcare research in less developed countries (Nuffield Council on Bioethics 2002; Schüklenk and Ashcroft 2000).

More recently, there have been attempts to formulate ethical frameworks to guide regulatory developments and scientific research in stem cell research. Even within the European Union, there are significant regulatory differences on the creation of human embryos for research, with the United Kingdom and Belgium permitting the creation of embryos for research, while in Germany, Austria and Ireland the creation of human embryos for research is banned (Harris, Bortolotti and Irving 2005: 158). What legal and ethical concerns, if any, arise when health researchers travel to another jurisdiction in order to undertake research that would be regulated or would not be permitted in their home jurisdiction? If a government in one country bans a particular type of research yet another country's laws permit it, how and where do we draw the boundary lines for law and for ethics? We need to consider the extent to which ethical standpoints are localized. We also need to consider what this means for the development of universal ethical principles and for the ways we might seek to regulate biomedical research at the supranational and international level (ibid.).

We could, for example, decide simply to tolerate the different regulatory approaches of individual countries. But this really depends on the nature of the research in question. For example, would we be tolerant of researchers proposing to attempt to clone a human, often referred to as 'reproductive cloning', or perhaps genetic manipulation of inheritable characteristics, on the basis that the jurisdiction in which they were located did not prohibit such research? One could easily imagine that there would be considerable consternation at such possibilities. Indeed, the international declarations that have been developed in recent years around the use of cloning technologies seem designed, at least in part, to head off such possibilities and to lay down some ethical principles of universal applicability.

Attempts are under way to find common ground and common ethical principles. In Europe, the EUROSTEM project has proposed an ethical framework that rests on the common acceptance of core principles, such as beneficence and respect-for-persons, while simultaneously recognizing that countries may have different interpretations over the scope of those principles. Under this framework, the different approaches to the meaning of respect-for-persons in relation to the embryo could still be expressed at a national level (ibid.: 160). The framework would also provide protection for

3 For discussion of the development of national and international guidelines on the conduct of health-care research, see Nuffield Council on Bioethics 2002: ch 5.

individual researchers engaging in collaborative work by proposing that 'no one working in the EU should be punished or rendered liable to prosecution, restriction or discrimination for undertaking research that is permitted in that country' (ibid.: 161). Finally, they recommend that any therapies developed from stem cell research be made widely available within the European Union in the hope that this will facilitate the development of a consensus (ibid.). Yet, as Harris et al. note (ibid.), the development and availability of stem cell-derived therapies would focus a new ethical dilemma for individuals and countries opposed to embryonic stem cell research: 'Does the unacceptability of the research entail the unacceptability of the therapies?'

The Hinxton Group, an international consortium of researchers on stem cells, ethics and law, has also sought to develop a consensus approach to the ethical dilemmas raised by stem cell research. Concerned that a diversity of regulatory approaches can hinder scientific collaboration and research, the Group has issued a consensus statement of ethical principles to guide regulatory development in the field of stem cell research. Like the EUROSTEM project, the Hinxton Group also recommends that individual researchers be free from prosecution, liability or discrimination provided they are conducting their research in accordance with the laws of the country in which they are located.

Disease, trade and tourism

Infectious diseases have played an important role in shaping human society. In the globalized world, that potential is greater than ever before. Yet although there are clear gaps and disparities between health and wealth in the developing and developed worlds, such distinctions are in part illusory, as infectious diseases are unlikely to remain confined only to the world's poor. The huge burden of infectious disease within the developing world will continue to pose a threat to the populations of both developing countries and the broader international community. With more than two million people crossing international borders every day and more than one million people travelling from developing to developed countries every week, the 'functional separation between domestic and international health problems is losing its usefulness' (Brundtland 2003: 420). As Gro Harlem Brundtland has commented, 'No impregnable walls exist between a world that is healthy, well-fed, and well-off and another that is sick, malnourished, and impoverished' (ibid.: 417).

Those of us who live in the developed world have tended to become somewhat complacent about the threats posed by infectious diseases. Although we know that the influenza epidemic in the years following the First World War killed millions of people, the risks posed by infectious disease seem increasingly remote for those of us living in the developed world. Many of the childhood diseases that threatened the lives of the young in previous generations have largely been overcome by childhood vaccination programmes. Yet in 2003, the emergence of a new respiratory disease that we now know as SARS (severe acute respiratory syndrome) provided a very clear reminder of the power of infectious diseases. The global spread of SARS demonstrated that infectious diseases do not recognize borders and in today's global community can spread quickly to affect all countries, both rich and poor (Bennett

2006). The current concerns over avian flu, discussed in Chapter 6, are another reminder of these issues.

While the recent revision of the International Health Regulations (IHR) will lead to a revitalized, formal framework within which the world community can respond to the threat of infectious disease to domestic and international economies and populations (ibid.), formal legal requirements are only one part of the solution and do little to address the circumstances and conditions within countries that contribute to the emergence of disease outbreaks. There is a real need for the international community to engage with the issue of infectious disease and develop a deeper understanding of the close relationship between international health and international prosperity. The globalized economy links us all in very clear and close ways. Diseases are great tourists. As long as people travel and engage in trade with each other, diseases will go along for the ride.

Fertility tourism

One of the best-known forms of health tourism is that associated with reproduction. Women have long travelled within and between countries in order to access the reproductive medical services they require. They have, for example, travelled from rural areas in order to access abortion services that are more readily available in cities, have travelled within countries from states with restrictive abortion laws to those with more liberal ones,[4] and have travelled internationally in order to access assisted conception.[5]

Writing on reproductive tourism in Europe, Guido Pennings has argued that the main causes of reproductive tourism are as follows: that the treatment is prohibited in the patient's country of origin; because the treatment is not available in the patient's home country due to lack of expertise; long waiting lists, or high financial costs (2004: 2690). Pennings has noted the extent of fertility tourism between European countries:

> The Belgian register of assisted reproduction for 1999 indicates that 30% of patients receiving *in vitro* fertilization come from aboard. When oocyte donation is considered separately, 60% of all recipients are foreigners...For preimplantation genetic diagnosis, half of the couples come from Germany and France as a result of legal or practical restrictions in these countries. [ibid.]

While fertility tourism is undoubtedly driven in part by regulatory requirements and restrictions, with individuals travelling to other jurisdictions with more liberal laws, within the European Union (EU) fertility tourism has also been shaped by

---

4 See Kreimer (1992: 453–4): 'about 40% of all legal abortions performed in the United States in 1972 were performed on women outside of their state of residence. Two years after *Roe,* only 13.4% of legal abortions involved women from another state, and by 1977 the figure had dropped below 10%.'

5 See Pennings (2004). As Canoles has noted, 'One European country could completely ban fertility procedures, yet if a neighboring country allows all fertility procedures, the banning country's prohibition is virtually meaningless' (2002: 201).

the intersections between national laws and EU laws. EU laws have been used to challenge an injunction that initially preventing a pregnant Irish girl from leaving the country for nine months, although the case was ultimately decided on constitutional grounds.[6] In 1997, the Court of Appeal in England held that Diane Blood's rights under European Community law had not been adequately taken into account when the Human Fertilisation and Embryology Authority (HFEA) initially decided that Mrs Blood could not be inseminated using her dead husband's sperm due to the requirement for written consent under English law. Following the decision of the Court of Appeal,[7] the HFEA granted Mrs Blood a licence allowing her to export the sperm to another country within the European Union. Mrs Blood was able to export her husband's sperm to Belgium and she subsequently had two sons (Blood 2005). The tensions that can arise in these cases between national and supranational forms of regulation typify the dynamics between the local and the global that arise in contemporary society, the regulatory challenges that arise from such dynamics,[8] and the ways in which laws designed to regulate free trade within federated unions can impact upon the national laws of individual member states (Hervey and McHale 2004: 153; Kreimer 1992; Phelan 1992).

Transplant tourism

Developments in organ donation and transplantation have provided important therapeutic options for those experiencing kidney failure or other conditions requiring an organ transplant. Unfortunately, in most countries, demand for organs far exceeds the available supply. It has been reported that just in Europe there are 40,000 people waiting for a kidney and 120,000 patients receiving dialysis treatment (Nullis-Kapp 2004). In most parts of Australia, patients wait on average for about four years for a kidney from a deceased donor (Mathew, Faull and Snelling 2005). The increasing demand for organs is also reportedly fuelling international trade in organs. It is reported that brokers are charging US$100,000–200,000 to arrange a transplant, while donors are likely to receive about US$5,000 for a kidney but may receive as little as US$1,000 (Nullis-Kapp 2004). With donors likely to be poor and ill-educated and recipients likely to be wealthy, the differences in wealth and opportunities are very clear, prompting one commentator to note that:

> In general, the circulation of kidneys follows established routes of capital from South to North, from East to West, from poorer to more affluent bodies, from black and brown bodies to white ones, and from female to male or from poor, low status men to more affluent men. Women are rarely the recipients of purchased organs anywhere in the world. [Scheper-Hughes 2003: 1645]

For individuals living in poverty in a poor country, the sale of a kidney or other body parts may seem like a solution to economic hardship. Indeed, it has been suggested

6 *Attorney General v. X* [1992] ILRM 401. For discussion see Hervey and McHale (2004: 152–3).

7 See *Ex parte Blood* [1997] 2 All ER 687 (CA). See also Blood (2005); Hervey (1998).

8 For discussion, see Chapter 1.

that 'The kidney as a commodity has emerged as the gold standard in the new body trade, representing the poor person's ultimate collateral against hunger, debt, and penury' (Scheper-Hughes 2003: 1645). Yet hopes of prosperity following the sale of a kidney may be illusory. One study of people in India who had sold their kidney reported that while most people sold their kidneys in order to pay off debts, family income declined for many of the participants in the study following nephrectomy and many participants were still in debt (Goyal et al. 2002). While some might argue that sellers have a right to make autonomous decisions over their bodies, most of the participants in the study indicated that they would not recommend selling a kidney (ibid.: 1591). The authors of the study concluded that the 'sale of kidneys by poor people in India does not lead to a tangible benefit for the seller' (ibid.: 1592). Interestingly, an Australian study indicates that overseas commercial kidney transplantations may also place the buyer at increased risk of lower survival rates and increased risk of infections (Kennedy et al. 2005).

In May 2004, the 57th World Health Assembly urged Member States 'to take measures to protect the poorest and vulnerable groups from "transplant tourism" and the sale of tissues and organs, including attention to the wider problem of international trafficking in human tissues and organs' (World Health Assembly 2004: Article 1(5)). The Assembly also requested the Director-General 'to provide support for Member States in their endeavours to prevent organ trafficking, including drawing up guidelines to protect the poorest and most vulnerable groups from being victims of organ trafficking' (Article 2(4)).

Although commercial trade in human tissue is prohibited in a number of jurisdictions, including Australia,[9] there is growing debate about the development of a possible market to meet the demand for organs (see, for example, Goodwin 2006; Wilkinson 2003). The increasing globalization of health care and the meeting of demand by wealthy patients with the desperation of local donors, and improved success rates for transplantation, feed the continued growth in organ trafficking which in turn erodes national taboos against commodification (Harrington 2006: 176). In the debate over the possibility of a market for organs, the logic of the liberal market comes into conflict with the ethics of global disparities in wealth and health. As John Harrington has noted:

> Regulation can indeed improve the likelihood and the quality of consent obtained from organ sellers. But it is itself dependent on the political and economic context in which it must operate...The ethics of organ markets inevitably implicate questions of social and global justice not readily fitted within the analytical grid of liberal bioethics. [2006: 177]

9 Human Tissue Act 1983 (NSW) s. 32; Transplantation and Anatomy Act 1978 (ACT) s. 44; Human Tissue Transplant Act 1979 (NT) s. 24; Transplantation and Anatomy Act 1979 (Qld) ss. 40–42; Transplantation and Anatomy Act 1983 (SA) s. 35; Human Tissue Act 1982 (Vic) ss. 38–9; Human Tissue and Transplant Act 1982 (WA) s. 29; Human Tissue Act 1985 (Tas) s. 27.

Between the Local and the Global: Defining Legal Limits

Each of the areas discussed above reveals the complexities of health within the global village. Increasingly, the pressing issues for global health policy arise at the interface between countries of differing wealth and resources. While identification of these issues is relatively straightforward, trying to work out how to respond to them in regulatory terms is a far more difficult issue. Typically, responses to the issues raised by health tourism revolve around the extraterritorial reach of local laws, around calls to harmonize laws, or around calls for recognition of legal pluralism. An analysis of these responses to the challenges posed by the diverse issues outlined above reveals the limitations and practical challenges associated with attempts to formulate regulatory responses.

Local laws and extraterritorial reach

Countries seeking to restrict their citizens' access to health tourism could seek to restrict the rights of their citizens to access or use certain activities while they are in other jurisdictions. Countries could seek to prevent citizens from travelling abroad to access prohibited services, impose domestic legal penalties on citizens who access prohibited services while abroad (Kreimer 1992: 458), or enact statutes with extraterritorial reach (Mehlman and Rabe 2002: 192–9). Within federal legal systems, the right to travel freely between states and interstate trade and commerce issues are typically issues of constitutional law rather than health law (Kreimer 1992). In reality, although there may be important legal issues that arise in relation to extraterritorial reach of laws, it is very difficult to see how they will make a real difference in curtailing fertility or transplant tourism – after all, in most instances, governments in individual countries are not likely to know that individual citizens have travelled abroad in order to access health services.

National and international legal harmonization

Despite the interplay between national and international laws, it is clear that the global nature of modern markets and professional and scientific communities also poses significant challenges for national regulation. Efforts by countries to limit or otherwise regulate biomedical activities within their borders are challenged by the practical realities and fluidity of the globalized economy in which business is conducted internationally, across national boundaries. While countries can endeavour to regulate medical science within their borders, the globalized world is a more permeable world, and the relevance of national laws becomes a far more complex matter than was once the case. Although medical science can be regulated within national boundaries, individuals, researchers or others may choose to relocate to another jurisdiction where the laws are less complex or less restrictive. While this perhaps drives an imperative towards the development of international standards and declarations, inconsistencies in laws at a national level create opportunities for what has been termed a form of regulatory forum shopping. Referring to 'a global market for assisted conception', Lee and Morgan have noted:

> Where technological development results in the blurring of national boundaries, the increasingly difficult task of one country insulating itself from events elsewhere in the world has given rise to the possibility of what has been called 'procreative tourism' and ethical dumping. [2001a: 307]

Discussion of health tourism and of the regulatory differences between countries often leads to calls for international harmonization of relevant laws. Certainly, the international community has sought to respond to the challenges posed by developments in medical science and in recent years we have seen a number of international declarations addressing these issues.[10] These international declarations can be seen as providing a framework for international harmonization. The international debates leading to such declarations play a positive role in fostering debate about developments in science and technology and the appropriate regulatory limits for such developments. Furthermore, international declarations and standards can play an important role in shaping the parameters for the development of laws and policies at a domestic level for individual countries (Opeskin 1998: 353–5).

There is a certain appeal about calls for harmonization. The idea that individual countries should work together to determine common ground and core areas of agreement so as to foster moves to more standardized forms of regulation is very appealing, particularly in the context of the current patchwork of national laws and policies. Choices would need to be made about whether to aim for harmonization of rules, harmonization of principles, or harmonization of institutional structures (Campbell and Nycum 2005: 135–41). Yet even once these choices have been made, harmonization is not without difficulties. The challenges include firstly, the need to avoid the 'lowest common denominator' effect, whereby agreement is only achieved at a minimal level and 'adhering to less stringent harmonized standards could involve the downgrading of domestic legal norms and requirements' (ibid.: 127). Secondly, cultural diversity may challenge attempts at harmonization (ibid.: 129), as international debates over stem cells and cloning technologies reveal. Finally, harmonization attempts will need to develop standards that have legitimacy and thus are more likely to have wide acceptance (ibid.: 130–31). Calls for harmonization also presuppose that it is possible to reach agreement on core principles and the direction in which harmonization should move. Guido Pennings has commented on these difficulties:

> The proponents of legislative harmonization seem to consider harmonization as a one-way movement: the others should adopt the same laws we have and they should forbid the same acts we forbid. It is obvious that when two parties start with this position in mind, they will not reach harmony. The direction of the 'harmonization', towards more limitations or towards more freedom, is crucial. [2004: 2692]

This analysis accurately captures the key dilemma in the development of international approaches to ethical challenges. In short, although we may seek to

---

10 See for example, UNESCO, Universal Declaration on the Human Genome and Human Rights (1997); Council of Europe's Convention on Human Rights and Biomedicine (1997). For discussion see Bell (1999).

develop harmonized approaches to regulatory values and systems, a key question is that of what values we are seeking to reflect. The debate over cloning reveals the challenges inherent in reaching international consensus and developing harmonized regulatory approaches. Even within Europe, there are real difficulties in formulating harmonized approaches around issues such as stem cell research. Those challenges are magnified when they move to the international stage.

Yet the prospects are not all gloomy. There are increasing moves to harmonize regulatory approaches across a range of areas and jurisdictions, particularly within regions. As discussed above, there have been attempts to begin the process of developing consensus around the ethically fraught area of stem cell research. Australia and New Zealand have sought to harmonize regulation in some areas[11] while within Europe, developments at the EC level can also play a harmonizing role on laws at the level of individual countries.

Legal pluralism and moral limits

The debates about health tourism are debates about the contemporary meanings of legal pluralism and the role of moral limits in shaping laws. Health tourism is often condemned as both the preserve of the wealthy and a means of exploitation of the poor. There is the question of equity and fairness in some individuals being able to travel to other jurisdictions to access the health services they want. As Hervey notes, this means that 'Citizens of the EU are in effect treated differently on the grounds of their ability to pay for privately remunerated reproductive services' (1998: 229). Millns makes a similar point when she comments:

> The practical implication of this triumph of the economic dimension of rights under EC law is that women seeking treatments (just like any other patients), once equipped with the necessary financial resources, can go health-care shopping in another member state, where the laws may be more lax. [2002: 33]

Travelling to another country in order to access health services is in fact likely to be an option that is only available to the financially secure, even in the developed countries of the world (Harrington 2006: 178). Yet given that costs of the health care being sought may be considerably lower in another country than it is in the patient's home country, it has been argued that health tourism may promote equity to some degree: 'reproductive tourism may actually reduce social injustice and unfairness by allowing poorer patients from rich countries to obtain the treatment they cannot afford in their home country' (Pennings 2004: 2691).

Health tourism is driven by factors such as cost and restrictive legislation. The ability of people to travel across borders in order to access health services may be seen as, to some extent at least, driving the move to harmonization or even liberalization of laws. In competitive economic climates, countries offering less restrictive regulatory environments may gain a competitive advantage over other states where research activities are subjected to greater regulation (Hervey 1998: 231), which may foster health tourism in a variety of different areas. These issues

11 See for example, Food Standards Australia New Zealand <www.foodstandards.gov.au>.

add new complexities to the setting of national regulatory agendas where local cultural and religious contexts may lead to different priorities from those that are purely or largely economic (ibid.: 230).

In a recent report, the Human Genetics Commission in the UK considered the issue of reproductive tourism and noted the concerns that had been expressed about the possible costs for the National Health Service that might arise if complications or side-effects arise after a person's return home. The Commission noted, 'While we are sympathetic to these concerns, the solutions available (for instance, refusing to treat or charging for the treatment) would not be just so long as the NHS provides treatment for injuries sustained during other risky pursuits such as skiing' (Human Genetics Commission 2006: para. 6.23).

Individual countries could develop their own domestic legislation aimed at discouraging health tourism if they felt strongly about it. Access to national health benefits could, for example, be denied to individuals who developed complications after accessing health services in countries where the safety standards were below those accepted in the home jurisdiction. Individual countries could also work together to develop complementary laws designed to restrict or discourage undesirable forms of health tourism both in countries from which the tourists originate and the destination countries. Yet it is important to realize that not all forms of health tourism might be regarded as undesirable. We would, for example, be unlikely to condemn someone who travelled to the US in order to access cutting-edge health care, such as a new treatment for a medical condition that was unavailable in their home country. We need to think very carefully then about our reasons for condemning or condoning health tourism. Furthermore, even if a state decides to prohibit or limit access to certain medical services within its borders, it is quite a different decision to try to restrict one's citizens from accessing such services when they are lawfully available in another jurisdiction.

How then are we to determine the best way of regulating these areas? While each of the issues discussed in this chapter seems to be very distinct and certainly does raise its own unique questions, there are a number of common themes. It is sensible to see if harmonized and consensus-based approaches to law can be developed. Yet as the recent UN declaration on cloning shows, such consensus is not always easy. Indeed, there is a need to recognize that despite moves towards harmonization of laws and policies at the regional and international level, that legal and ethical pluralism is part of the landscape for contemporary society and likely to remain so. In this context, the relationship between the local and the global is one that will continue to be played out in the shaping of laws and policies at the national and international level. While we may be able to develop harmonized regulatory approaches to some issues, for other issues harmonization may be difficult or even impossible to achieve. We may, for example, find it easier to reach agreement around the setting of benchmarks for safety standards yet much harder to reach agreement around those issues, such as stem cell research, that raise complex ethical or moral issues. A key part of moving forward to the future will be to accept the place of pluralism in contemporary global society. In the United Kingdom, the House of Commons Science and Technology Committee's report, *Human Reproductive Technologies and the Law*, acknowledged this viewpoint, commenting:

> Charters, declarations and treaties no doubt keep diplomats busy and fulfilled but there are some ethical issues which are the domain of nation states and cultures. We should respect the cultures and desires of others and not seek to impose our own ideas. Such charters can only produce vague, lowest common-denominator agreements that are of questionable clarity and dubious effectiveness. Further attempts should be resisted until legislation and regulation are more widespread and the common threads can be identified. [2005: para. 387]

Finally, recognition of pluralism is not an excuse for 'anything goes'. International human rights discourse is premised on the idea of common values. Assessments of health tourism need to rest on such values and rights. In assessing the ethics of particular forms of health tourism, it will be necessary to assess the extent to which the rights of all parties are respected and protected. When we are trying to work out whether to condone or condemn particular forms of health tourism, we should seek to determine whether the tourism in question is consistent with respecting the human rights of the individuals concerned. In this sense then, the context is all important as is the relationship between health and human rights. In assessing the ethics of health tourism and its challenges for law, it is impossible to lump all forms of travel for health purposes into one category that is to be condemned. Instead, we need to ensure that we develop more nuanced responses so that we can more accurately assess and judge the links between health, travel and human rights.

Chapter 6

Globalization and Public Health Law

> Shall I say we rejoiced as the conviction grew in man and beast that the Plague was truly gone from us? No, we did not rejoice. For the losses were too many and the damage to our spirits too profound. For every one of us who still walked upon the Earth, two of us lay under it. Everywhere we went, we passed the sorry, makeshift graves of our friends and neighbours.
>
> Geraldine Brooks, *Year of Wonders: A Novel of the Plague*, p. 255

Year of Wonders (Brooks, 2002) tells the story of Anna Frith, a young woman with a husband and two small children living in a small village in rural England in 1665. When her husband Sam is killed in a mining accident, Anna finds it hard to make ends meet. When George Viccars, a quietly spoken journeyman tailor knocks on her door one day looking for lodging, Anna quickly agrees to rent him her attic room for sixpence a week. Anna and George become close and it appears that romance may blossom between them.

One day, when Anna returns from her work at the village rectory, she is surprised that George is not sitting stitching by the fire as usual. She finds him laying in his bed burning with fever. As Anna nurses her sick lodger she sees the huge painful swelling that has developed in George's neck, growing larger and more painful to touch until it finally bursts, 'splitting like a pea pod and issuing forth creamy pus all spotted through with shreds of dead flesh' (ibid.: 43). George Viccars died during the second night of his illness, the first victim of bubonic plague to strike the small village.

As fear of plague strikes, some flee the village. Concerned that such flight will simply spread the disease to neighbouring towns, the rector convinces the villagers to place themselves in quarantine. Necessary supplies are delivered by a neighbouring town and left at a boundary stone at the limits of the village. In the months that follow, one villager after another sickens and dies from plague. As the death toll mounts, there are too many dead for them to be buried in the churchyard and they are buried on unconsecrated land near where they died. During 1666, the plague reaps its deadly toll, leaving the villagers grief stricken and fearful of their neighbours. Some villagers turn to charms to ward off the plague, others to religion, some to violence and some 'slaked their dread in drink and their loneliness in wanton caresses' (ibid.: 218). Gradually the plague passes, leaving the village much diminished in population and the remaining villagers emotionally exhausted.

Although a work of fiction, *Year of Wonders* is based on the true story of the village of Eyam in Derbyshire, England during an outbreak of plague in 1666. The disease is probably best known as the Black Death and for the outbreak that killed up to a quarter of Europe's population in the mid-fourteenth century (Diamond 1998: 202). Facilitated by renewed networks of trade, that meant 'that even the most remote parts [of Europe] had become part of a single disease pool' (Kelly 2004: 27), plague swept across medieval Europe decimating local populations and sparking fear and panic.

By the beginning of the twentieth century, the link between plague and the bacterium that causes it (*yersinia pestis*) had been established (Marriott 2002). It is now known that plague is a disease carried by small animals and their fleas, and is transmitted to humans and animals through the bites of infected fleas, through direct contact with infective materials, and through inhalation (World Health Organisation 2005a).[1] With the introduction of de-ratting programmes and other public health measures, outbreaks of plague became less common. Although there are still outbreaks of plague, the toll from such outbreaks is far removed from the widespread death of the Middle Ages.[2] Nevertheless, the disease still carries with it a powerful symbolism of rapid death and still has the potential to cause widespread panic.

The story of the plague and humanity's quest to understand its cause, and to put in place preventative measures against further outbreaks, is part of a broader story of the relationship between humanity, globalization and infectious diseases (Marriott 2002: 111–12). It is a story that has been told through the ages and that continues to be told today as the global community confronts the emergence of new infectious diseases such as SARS, Ebola and HIV, while at the same time it struggles to conquer older diseases such as tuberculosis and malaria.

The Pandemic Threat

In 2003, the World Health Organisation described severe acute respiratory syndrome (SARS) as 'the first severe and readily transmissible new disease to emerge in the twenty-first century' (2003a: 1). The emergence of SARS as a global concern in early 2003 focused international attention on the threat posed by infectious diseases and the state of global preparedness for pandemic disease (Bennett 2006; Fidler 2004). By July 2003, when the World Health Organisation announced the interruption of human-to-human transmission of SARS (2003b), the disease had spread to 29 countries, causing 8,098 cases of the disease and 774 deaths (World Health Organisation 2003c). Some countries were hit particularly hard by SARS, with China, Hong Kong, Taiwan, Singapore, Vietnam, and Toronto in Canada all experiencing clusters of cases (Lee et al. 2003; Pang et al. 2003; Poutanen et al. 2003; Tsang et al. 2003; World Health Organisation 2003c). David Fidler has argued that 'SARS posed a public health governance challenge the likes of which modern public health had not previously

---

1 There are three forms of plague: (i) bubonic, which is the most common form and is contracted by a bite from an infected flea. In the bubonic form the lymph nodes become inflamed (forming buboes); (ii) septicaemic, where the plague bacteria spreads through the bloodstream; and (iii) pneumonic, which is the least common form, and can be transmitted from person to person (World Health Organisation 2005a).

2 The World Health Organisation has recorded 38,310 cases of plague (with 2,845 deaths) in 25 countries in the period from 1989 to 2003. Three geographical areas have experienced outbreaks of plague over the past decade: India (1994: 2002), Indonesia (1997) and Algeria (2003) (World Health Organisation 2005d).

confronted' (2004: 6) because of its global spread, its ability for human-to-human transmission, and the lack of an effective vaccine or treatment.

The emergence of SARS led to global panic which in turn increased the impact of SARS on the economies of affected countries. In Canada, it was estimated that tourism lost $350 million, that reduced airport activity cost $220 million and that non-tourism retail sales reduced by $380 million (National Advisory Committee on SARS and Public Health 2003: 211). In China, public entertainment venues and schools were closed in an effort to limit spread of the disease (Pang et al. 2003: 3219). Health systems in the most affected countries struggled under the sudden strain. Many health professionals became ill during the early stages of the disease (National Advisory Committee on SARS and Public Health 2003: 41; Pang et al. 2003: 3217; Cameron, Rainer and Smit 2003), and there was increased demand for medical supplies and hospital beds, all of which highlighted the need for health systems to have 'surge capacity' (National Advisory Committee on SARS and Public Health 2003: 102).

While SARS was a new disease and its emergence unexpected, it seems to be only a matter of time before we experience the next, perhaps deadly, pandemic. Influenza will likely be the culprit. Influenza pandemics have been documented since the sixteenth century. In the period since, there have been an average of three pandemics each century, at 10–50-year intervals (World Health Organisation 2005b: 23). In past centuries, pandemics 'have typically hit world populations like the epidemiological equivalent of a flash flood' (ibid.). Pandemics are characterized by a rapid global spread of the disease and by their capacity to make more than a quarter of the population ill (ibid.).

The influenza pandemic of 1918 killed at least 40 million people world-wide. The outbreak was particularly deadly, killing 'more people in a year than the Black Death of the Middle Ages killed in a century; it killed more people in 24 weeks than AIDS has killed in 24 years' (Barry 2004: 5). The disease caused far more deaths than the estimated 8.3 million military deaths during the First World War (World Health Organisation 2005b: 25) and was the third most deadly recorded pandemic, after the outbreaks of plague in the sixth and fourteenth centuries (International Monetary Fund 2006: 4). Although influenza generally strikes hardest at society's weakest members – infants and the elderly – the 1918 flu was different. In the 1918 outbreak, young adults were those most likely to die from the flu (Barry 2004: 239) – 99 per cent of deaths were in people under the age of 65 (World Health Organisation 2005b: 25). Pneumonia is a recognized secondary complication of influenza. In the 1918 outbreak, the disease also caused a severe primary viral pneumonia that could be fatal. Although widespread quarantine and isolation measures were imposed, they could do little to stop the eventual spread of disease (ibid.). It is estimated that eventually 25–30 per cent of the world's population caught influenza (ibid.: 26). The demographic impact of the disease was such that 'in many areas, life expectancy dropped by 10 years and more' (ibid.). While we will never know for sure exactly how many people died, it is possible that the 1918 pandemic killed five per cent of the world's young adults, with the figure nearing 10 per cent in less developed countries (Barry 2004: 398). Recent research calculating the excess mortality during the 1918–20 pandemic reveals a 30-fold variation in population mortality across countries (Murray et al. 2006) revealing the potential for significant global disparities in the impact of pandemic influenza.

In 1957, a pandemic of Asian influenza was caused by the H2N2 virus. This pandemic was milder than the deadly 1918 virus and influenza vaccines were available for seasonal flu epidemics, while antibiotics helped to treat complications from flu (World Health Organisation 2005b: 26). Globally, the total excess mortality associated with the 1957 outbreak is estimated at more than two million deaths (ibid.: 29). In 1968, an influenza pandemic, caused by the H3N2 virus, led to global excess mortality of an estimated one million deaths (ibid.: 31). It is likely that the mildness of the 1968 pandemic can be explained in part by the genetic similarity of the 1968 virus to the viruses causing previous pandemics, meaning that at least some of the population probably had some protection against the disease (ibid.).

During 2004, outbreaks of avian flu in poultry in parts of Asia caused concern about the next pandemic. Indeed, in 2005 the World Health Organisation warned that 'The world has moved closer to a pandemic than at any time since 1968' (ibid.: 41). Avian influenza, an infectious disease of birds, was first identified over a hundred years ago. Migratory waterfowl are the natural reservoir of avian influenza and provide a mobile reservoir of the disease (ibid.: 36). In 1997 in Hong Kong, the H5N1 strain of avian influenza infected eighteen people, killing six (ibid.: 8). The source of human infection was discovered to be close contact with infected live poultry. Within three days, Hong Kong's entire poultry population was destroyed in an effort to avert further spread of the disease (ibid.).

In January 2004, severe respiratory disease hospitalized eleven children in Hanoi. Seven of the children died of the disease and the H5N1 virus was identified in specimens from two of the fatal cases (ibid.: 9, 11). In the following weeks, large outbreaks of highly pathogenic avian influenza caused by H5N1 were identified in poultry, mainly in Vietnam (ibid.: 11). Since 2003, avian influenza (H5N1) has infected more than 330 people globally, killing more than 200 (World Health Organisation 2007).

Influenza A viruses, of which avian influenza is a variety, are a particular public health concern as they mutate more quickly than influenza B viruses. Influenza A viruses also have a large number of subtypes and have the potential to infect birds, pigs and other animals (World Health Organisation 2005b: 10). Of particular concern is the potential for both antigenic drift and antigenic shift. In antigenic drift, small uncorrected errors that occur as the virus copies itself lead to constant changes in the genetic make-up of the virus, which in turn are able to evade the immune systems of individuals who do not have protection against the new strain of the virus. In antigenic shift, genetic segments of the virus can be swapped for the genetic segments of another influenza virus creating a new hybrid virus which will be completely new to the human immune system (ibid.).

The avian flu outbreak has highlighted concerns about the next influenza pandemic. It has been noted that the global spread of pandemic influenza has generally taken six to eight months, with the disease spreading along sea lanes (ibid.: 19), although with the speed of modern international travel it is possible that pandemic influenza could spread to all continents in less than three months (International Monetary Fund 2006: 12). As experience with SARS shows, international air travel can facilitate the rapid international spread of disease. This capacity, along with the infectious nature of influenza could pose major challenges for public health responses: 'Many of the public health interventions that successfully contained SARS will not be effective against a disease that is far more contagious, has a short incubation period, and can be transmitted before the onset of symptoms' (World Health Organisation 2005c: 4).

There is little doubt that we will experience another pandemic. The question is not if, but when. Yet it is difficult to predict the shape and consequences of the next pandemic. The world's population is much greater than in previous pandemics, while nutritional status of populations, medical treatments and global surveillance and response mechanisms have all greatly improved (World Health Organisation 2005b: 43). On the other hand, the global disparities in access to health services are much greater than they were a century ago, while the impact of pandemic influenza in a world where millions are infected with HIV remains unclear (ibid.).

The reaction to pandemic flu 'will change the world overnight' (Osterholm 2005: 418). International trade and travel are likely to be affected as countries introduce measures in an effort to prevent the virus from spreading to their territory, vaccine supplies would only be sufficient for a fraction of the world's population (even once a vaccine for the pandemic strain becomes available), and the global economy would be at risk:

> The global economy has never been measurably threatened by human immunodeficiency virus (HIV), malaria or tuberculosis despite the dramatic impact of these diseases on developing-world populations, particularly sub-Saharan Africa. The global panic created by flu will be different. Today, we have virtually no surge capacity for any consumer product or medical service that might be needed during the 12 to 36 months of a pandemic. [ibid.]

Pandemic influenza could have a dramatic effect on the global economy. The extent of the economic impact would depend on the severity of the pandemic, mortality rates, the degree of preparedness in health systems, and the response of households and businesses (International Monetary Fund 2006: 3). High rates of absenteeism from work during a pandemic, disruption to businesses and services, and reduced consumer demand and investment, could all contribute to the economic impact of a pandemic (ibid.). Reductions in tourism and the impact of trade and travel restrictions will also contribute to the economic impact (ibid.: 3–4). It has been estimated that a mild pandemic, similar to the 1968–69 Hong Kong flu, would cause 1.4 million deaths world-wide and that the global economy would shrink by 0.8 per cent of GDP (or about US$330 billion) (McKibbin and Sidorenko 2006). Murray et al. (2006) have estimated that an influenza pandemic similar to that of 1918–20 would cause an estimated 62 million deaths, with 96 per cent of these in the developing world. If we experience a pandemic worse than the 1918 Spanish flu, the pandemic could lead to more than 142 million deaths world-wide and cost the global economy US$4.4 trillion, or 12.6 per cent of GDP, with some economies, particularly in the developing world, shrinking by as much as 50 per cent (McKibbin and Sidorenko 2006: 26).

What is clear is that 'health systems around the world will be confronted by a sudden and sharp increase in the demand for health care' (World Health Organisation 2005b: 43). In Australia, it has been estimated that an influenza pandemic that affected 25 per cent of the Australian population and for which there was no available vaccine or treatment would lead to 13,000–44,000 deaths, 57,900–148,000 hospitalizations, and 2.6–7.5 million outpatient visits over a six to eight week period (Department of Health and Ageing 2005: 27). An influenza pandemic will present major logistical challenges in responding to the crisis. There will be a need for plans on how to equip and staff temporary hospitals, how to deal with the number of dead bodies, and how to decide on priority setting for the distribution of limited antiviral drugs (Osterholm 2005: 418). As part of their pandemic planning, health systems will also need to consider the relationships between hospitals and other elements of critical community infrastructure (such as power, telecommunications, water) that hospitals rely upon in order to function effectively (Itzwerth et al. 2006). If large populations around the world are affected almost simultaneously, it may be difficult to provide assistance of the kind that the international community is usually able to provide when one country or region experiences an humanitarian crisis (World Health Organisation 2005b: 43–4).

The Birth and Rebirth of Public Health

Infectious diseases and the risk of pandemic disease highlight the need for effective public health infrastructure. In the nineteenth century, the implementation of public health measures was fuelled by the need to respond to epidemic diseases within industrial cities (Porter 1997: 420). Tuberculosis, smallpox, sexually transmitted diseases and typhoid all became the focus of sanitary reform measures (ibid.: 420–25). Improved nutrition in the population and the introduction of public health measures combined to improve mortality figures in the population (ibid.: 426). Large-scale public health works, including the construction of sewage systems and water supplies all contributed to significant improvements in public health and in life expectancy (Mackenbach 2007).

There has also been a close connection between colonization and medicine, a connection that sparked a new branch of 'tropical medicine' (Porter 1997: 462). Throughout the eighteenth and nineteenth century, Europeans were exposed to diseases to which they had little or no previous contact through international trade and colonization in Africa, Asia and the Americas (ibid.: 464). Infectious disease thus provided an impediment to European attempts to colonize tropical areas (Diamond 1998: 214). Yet disease and Western medicine were also an important aspect of European colonization. Disease 'devastated and demoralized indigenous populations...clearing the way for European conquest' (Porter 1997: 482). Although colonization brought Western medicine to developing countries, 'The good that Western medicine did was marginal and incidental' (ibid.). In contrast, the disruption brought about by colonization also helped to spread disease to previously unaffected areas (ibid.: 465).

> Epidemiological link-ups between previously isolated regions, the movements of fleets and armies, of millions of slaves and indentured labourers, the spread of disease by ecological change and social dislocation, the misery bred by shanty-towns – all have been implicated in the hail of death that European rule brought. [ibid.: 482]

The nineteenth century also saw the birth of public health measures at an international level. During that century, there were ten international sanitary conferences, and eight international conventions in an effort to prevent or limit the international spread of infectious disease (World Health Organisation 2002b: 1). In 1892, a convention on cholera was adopted and in 1897 a convention on plague was adopted. These conventions would lay the groundwork for the International Health Regulations which would be developed in the mid-twentieth century. Key international organizations, including the International Sanitary Bureau, the Pan American Sanitary Bureau, the Office International d'Hygiène Publique, the Health Organization of the League of Nations and the Office International des Epizooties, were also established during this period (Fidler 2004: 78; World Health Organisation 2002b).

During the twentieth century, improvements in epidemiology, antimicrobial treatments and medicine generally delivered even more improvements in public health, fostering a complacency, at least in the developed countries of the world, that infectious diseases could be conquered (Fidler 2005: 335; Selgelid 2005: 284–5). In time, it became clear that the battle against infectious diseases had not been won after all. New infectious diseases continued to emerge, presenting new challenges for public health systems. In the past 30 years, at least 30 new infectious diseases have been identified, including SARS, avian flu, HIV and Ebola (Kindhauser 2003: 56). Nearly 40 million people are infected with HIV, mainly in sub-Saharan Africa. Some older infectious diseases, including tuberculosis, have also become increasingly drug-resistant. Approximately two million people die each year from tuberculosis and one-third of the world's population is infected with the disease (DeAngelis and Flanagin 2005). Furthermore, the growth of modern airline travel provided infectious diseases with new and efficient means of spreading internationally, as infected passengers could readily travel from one continent to another before they even realized that they were ill (Frenk and Gómez-Dantés 2002: 95). This capacity for international travel to facilitate the international spread of infectious diseases was borne out most recently in 2003 during the SARS crisis. Indeed, as a Canadian report noted, 'SARS has illustrated that we are constantly a short flight away from serious epidemics' (National Advisory Committee on SARS and Public Health 2003: 10).

Humanitarian crises can also provide an ideal setting for the emergence of diseases. In areas of conflict, a number of risk factors for communicable diseases may interact, including the dislocation and temporary resettlement of large numbers of people, overcrowded conditions, poverty, lack of access to safe water, inadequate sanitation, food shortages, and poor access to health care (Connolly et al. 2004: 1974). These factors may be further complicated by the collapse of public health infrastructure, unstable governments, difficulties in accessing affected populations due to conflict or insecurity, inadequate supplies of drugs and other requirements, and poor coordination between multiple agencies. Without appropriate communicable disease interventions in such emergencies these crises could provide the ground for a resurgence of old diseases (ibid.). Such areas also 'represent important potential zones of new disease emergence because of delays in detection and characterisation of new pathogens and their widespread transmission before control measures can be implemented' (ibid.: 1975). In addition, delays in detecting, reporting and containing epidemics present a threat to other countries both regionally and globally, while the continued presence of diseases targeted for eradication poses a threat to those goals and the investment therein (ibid.).

Climate and geography can also have the potential to impact upon human health. Factors such as temperature, rainfall and humidity all play a role in mosquito reproduction and thus influence mosquito-borne diseases such as malaria (Department of Health and Ageing 2004: 8). The frequency of droughts, water and soil usage and agricultural activities may all be affected by climate change through global warming (Juss 1997).

The growing realization that it is impossible for any one nation to isolate itself from infectious diseases has led to a renewed interest in public health and public health laws in the developed countries of the world and a growing recognition of the need to take a globalized approach to contemporary public health challenges. In the developed countries of the world, there is an increased focus on the continued threat from infectious diseases and on the need to formulate appropriate public health strategies in response. Public health laws remain a key element in such strategies.

Public Health Law and Ethics

The development of an effective public health infrastructure requires three key ingredients – health, law and ethics. Firstly, in relation to health, there is a need for a skilled workforce of health and medical professionals and the development and implementation of effective surveillance systems for emerging public health issues and emergencies. Secondly, there is the need for effective legal rules that set out the various rights and duties that arise in the public health context. At the global level, these laws are expressed through the International Health Regulations, while at the local level, public health rights and duties may be formalized in public health laws at the national, state or local levels. Thirdly, but by no means least, is the need for an ethical understanding of public health that can provide a moral and ethical framework for decision-making and choices at both the infrastructural and regulatory levels.

Public health laws are 'the inseparable companion of the public health process' (Reynolds 2004: 3). Larry Gostin has defined public health law as:

> the study of the legal powers and duties of the state to assure the conditions for people to be healthy (e.g. to identify, prevent, and ameliorate risks to health in the population) and the limitations on the power of the state to constrain the autonomy, privacy, liberty, proprietary, or other legally protected interests of individuals for protection or promotion of community health. [2000: 4]

At the heart of contemporary public health law is the weighing of individual and community interests. Public health measures have economic costs associated with implementing, enforcing and complying with public health regulations, and personal burdens arising from restrictions on individual autonomy or interference with proprietary interests (ibid.: 100–107). Quarantine and isolation can conflict with individuals' freedom of movement while surveillance and contact tracing may conflict with individuals' privacy rights. For these reasons, public health measures clearly do have the potential to come into conflict with individual autonomy.

In the second half of the twentieth century, several changes combined to bring about a reconceptualization and reorientation of public health (Childress and Bernheim 2003: 1196). Firstly, rights of privacy, liberty and due process began to be formalized in laws, including health laws relating to medical treatment in areas such as abortion, life-sustaining treatment and treatment of people with mental illness (ibid.). Secondly, infectious diseases no longer appeared to pose a major threat. Thirdly, the development of 'AIDS exceptionalism' whereby 'AIDS was generally exempted from some of the traditional public health measures, including quarantine' contributed to increased assertions of the link between health and human rights (ibid.).

> Focused on the centrality of education for mass behavioural change, the protection of the rights and privacy of people infected with HIV, and a rejection of coercive measures, the approach to AIDS was voluntarist at its core. A simple dictum emerged: no public health policy that violated the rights of individuals could be effective in controlling the spread of HIV. [Bayer and Fairchild 2004: 478]

While the reformulation of health rights that occurred around HIV marked the beginning of a new understanding of public health, 'those committed to a health and human rights perspective saw the new articulation as having broader implications for public health more generally' (ibid.: 479). In the current climate, the nature of public health ethics has again become an important issue and there is a growing recognition of the need for bioethics to see infectious disease as a topic of importance (Selgelid 2005). This development is driven by two trends. Firstly, in the wake of SARS, heightened fears of bioterrorism and concerns over the next outbreak of pandemic influenza, public health and public health law is again under scrutiny (Gostin 2002). Isolation and quarantine, both traditional tools in the fight against infectious diseases, were used in the face of the SARS outbreak in a number of countries including China, Hong Kong and Canada (Bayer and Fairchild 2004: 483). SARS demanded a rethink of public health ethics precisely because of the challenge it posed to effective containment responses. Secondly, as discussed in earlier chapters, the globalization of bioethics as a discipline, brought about by demands for distributive justice, particularly in the context of the 10/90 gap in medical research and the issue of access to essential medicines in the developing world, has focused attention on the public health needs of the developing world (see Selgelid 2005).

Global Preparedness

The World Health Organisation (WHO) has been working to improve global preparedness for influenza. The WHO has had an influenza surveillance programme since 1947. This programme is a network of laboratories around the world which analyse and track changes in the influenza virus. Today, the network comprises 113 national influenza centres in 84 countries and four WHO collaborating centres for influenza reference and research (World Health Organisation 2005b: 34).

In May 2005, the World Health Assembly approved a revised version of the International Health Regulations. In 1951, the Member States of the WHO adopted the International Sanitary Regulations. In 1969, the Regulations were renamed the

International Health Regulations (IHR), and were subsequently modified in 1973, 1981 and in 2005, with the revised IHR taking effect from 2007.

The IHR developed out of the international sanitary conventions held in the nineteenth century to address infectious diseases. David Fidler has called the period from the international sanitary conventions to the adoption of the International Sanitary Regulations in 1951 the 'classical regime' (2005: 328). Fidler describes the classical regime as one that

> ...established an international surveillance system for certain infectious diseases and attempted to harmonize national quarantine policies and regulations. The goal was to structure State responses to infectious disease outbreaks in other countries so that States could protect themselves from disease importation and spread in ways that were scientifically effective and the least restrictive of trade and travel possible. [ibid.: 330]

According to Fidler, the decline of the classical regime during the period from 1951 to 1981 was contributed to by four factors. First, the establishment of the World Health Organisation in 1948 provided a new context for global health, with the WHO focusing its efforts on disease eradication at local levels and promoting universal primary health care (ibid.: 334). Secondly, as developed countries made inroads into the burden of infectious disease through improvements in clean water, sanitation, and vaccines, their interest in the classical regime waned (ibid.: 335). Third, although the IHR did address vaccination requirements by States, the IHR did not require the use of vaccines for public health. Consequently, with the development of antibiotics and vaccines in the period after the Second World War and efforts to use these developments to fight infectious diseases globally, the IHR seemed less relevant (ibid.). Finally, there were ongoing problems of compliance with the ISR and the IHR; the IHR had become outdated and did not cover many infectious diseases, while the emergence of international human rights law (with a focus on a right to health), international trade law (which governed trade-restricting health measures), and international environmental law (which addressed non-communicable diseases) all contributed to the decline in the classical regime's role in international public health law (ibid.: 335–7). In 1981, smallpox was removed from the list of diseases covered by the IHR following its eradication in the 1970s. According to Fidler, this change to the IHR 'represents, in microcosm, the classical regime's marginalization and stagnation. The ISR and IHR made little, if any, contribution to the global eradication of smallpox – one of the greatest public health achievements in human history' (ibid.: 337–8).

The 20-year period from 1981 to 2001 represented the death of the classical regime as the IHR became increasingly irrelevant in the face of the emergence of the devastating HIV/AIDS pandemic, the emergence of new infectious diseases, the re-emergence of older diseases and the proliferation of biological weapons (ibid.: 338). In 1995, the revision of the IHR began when the World Health Assembly requested the Director-General of the WHO to revise and update the IHR (ibid.: 344; World Health Organisation 2002b). The revisions of the IHR were finalized in 2005, taking effect from 2007.

The IHR set out the obligations of WHO Member States in relation to notification of infectious diseases, the health measures that countries should take at ports and airports, and the maximum measures that countries may take during disease outbreaks. Article 2 of the IHR (2005) states that the purpose and scope of the Regulations are 'to prevent, protect against, control and provide a public health response to the international spread of disease in ways that are commensurate with and restricted to public health risks, and which avoid unnecessary interference with international traffic and trade'.

The IHR (2005) require Member States to establish a National IHR Focal Point to implement the public health measures required by the Regulations (Article 4(1)). Countries are required to 'develop, strengthen and maintain' the capacity to 'detect, assess, notify and report' public health events of international concern (Article 5, Annex 1). The WHO will assist countries to develop and maintain these capacities if requested to do so (Article 5(3)).

The revised IHR also expressly give the WHO the authority to collect information about events from its own surveillance activities and to assess whether the event has the potential to spread internationally or to interfere with international traffic (Article 5(4)). Article 9 of the revised IHR provides that the 'WHO may take into account reports from sources other than notifications or consultations.' The WHO is required to assess such reports according to established epidemiological principles and then communicate the information to the relevant state. The WHO is also required to attempt to verify the event with the relevant state before taking any action based on the report. These provisions clearly envisage the WHO making use of non-state sources of information about infectious disease outbreaks. Even before the revision of the IHR, the WHO had been using GOARN (the Global Outbreak Alert and Response Network), to link existing networks and GPHIN (Global Public Health Intelligence Network) in identifying public health events that could potentially be of global significance (World Health Organisation 2003a: 4). The inclusion of non-state actors in the governance of global public health is an important addition to the IHR for it 'changes the surveillance dynamic between WHO and Member States in ways that favour global health security over national sovereignty' (Fidler 2005: 376).

Member States must assess events within its territory using a decision instrument contained in the IHR in order to assess whether an event within their territory constitutes a public health emergency of international concern. Certain listed diseases, including SARS and smallpox, must be notified to the WHO. For other events, countries are required to assess them according to an algorithm that requires the assessment of events in terms of whether they are serious, unusual, or unexpected, whether there is a significant risk of international spread, or whether there is a significant risk of international travel or trade restrictions. If the answer to any of these questions is yes, then the event must be notified to the WHO under the IHR.

If there is an unexpected or unusual public health event within a country that could be a public health emergency of international concern, the country is required to provide the WHO with 'all relevant public health information' (Article 7). If there is an event within a country that does not require notification under the IHR, such as where there is insufficient information in order to be able to complete the IHR decision instrument, a country may keep the WHO advised and consult on the health measures that should be taken (Article 8). In such circumstances, the WHO will not make the information available to other countries until it has been confirmed that the event is a public health emergency of international concern; or international spread of the disease has been confirmed by the WHO; or there is evidence that 'control measures against the international spread are unlikely to succeed because of the nature of the contamination, disease agent, vector or reservoir'; or that the country lacks the capacity to implement steps to prevent further spread of the disease, or that 'immediate application of international control measures' is needed (Article 11). The WHO is required to consult with the relevant country about its intention relating to making available information about a public health event within the country (Article 11(3)). The WHO is able to make information available to the public if the public health event has already become public knowledge 'and there is a need for the dissemination of authoritative and independent information' (Article 11(4)).

In determining whether a public health emergency of international concern exists, the Director-General of the WHO is required to consider: information received from the relevant country; the decision instrument contained in the IHR; the advice of the Emergency Committee, comprised of experts, which is established in accordance with Articles 48 and 49 of the IHR; scientific principles, and 'an assessment of the risk to human health, of the risk of international spread of disease and of the risk of interference with international traffic' (Article 12(4)). If there is a public health emergency of international concern, the Director-General can issue temporary (Article 15) or standing (Article 16) recommendations in accordance with the procedures set out in the IHR to reduce the international spread of disease while avoiding 'unnecessary interference with international traffic'. The criteria for considering temporary or standing recommendations are set out in Article 17.

Like the previous IHR, the revised IHR set out public health measures to be taken at ports and airports in relation to travellers. Countries can implement health measures that give a greater degree of protection than the IHR provided the measures are consistent with the Regulations (Article 43(1)). Countries are required to base their public health measures on scientific principles and evidence and 'any available specific guidance or advice from WHO' (Article 43(2)). Countries implementing additional public health measures 'which significantly interfere with international traffic' are required to provide the WHO with the public health rationale and the scientific information for such measures (Article 43(3)). The WHO may ask a country to reconsider such measures after it has assessed the information provided by the country and other relevant information (Article 43(4)).

The revision of the IHR is a significant development in international health law. The previous IHR, which had been in force since 1969, were disease-specific, requiring countries to provide notifications only of certain specified infectious diseases (plague, cholera and yellow fever). By contrast, the new IHR contain a broad definition of disease, defining it as 'an illness or medical condition, irrespective of origin or source, that presents or could present significant harm to humans' (IHR (2005), Article 1(1)). Since this definition of disease covers all diseases 'irrespective of origin or source' it is not limited to naturally occurring conditions. This means, as Fidler and Gostin point out, that the public health risks covered by the new IHR include:

> (1) naturally occurring infectious diseases, whether of known or unknown etiological origin; (2) the potential international spread of non-communicable diseases caused by chemical or radiological agents in products moving in international commerce; and (3) suspected intentional or accidental releases of biological, chemical, or radiological substances. [2006: 86–7]

Furthermore, the focus on public health emergencies of international concern represents a move away from a narrow disease-specific focus and towards a more flexible and responsive IHR with risks to human health at the centre. As Fidler and Gostin note, 'Trade calculations determined the old IHR's scope, but risks to human health define the new IHR's scope' (ibid.: 87). The revised IHR also recognize the contemporary relevance of international human rights for international public health (Fidler 2005: 367). Article 3(1) provides that implementation of the IHR 'shall be with full respect for the dignity, human rights and fundamental freedoms of persons'.

There is no doubt that the revised IHR represent an important and long-overdue development in global public health law. However, the new IHR will not be sufficient on their own to tackle the problem of the global spread of infectious disease. Although the IHR require States to identify and respond to public health emergencies, they do not require States to be proactive in addressing the conditions that foster disease. As Fidler notes, the revised IHR 'are rules for global disease triage rather than global disease prevention' (ibid.: 389). Non-compliance by States also helped to bring about the end of the previous IHR. The new IHR may face similar challenges with non-compliance, although the potential for this may be somewhat limited now with the development of the Internet and the enormous difficulties States face in keeping disease outbreaks secret (ibid.: 389–90). Under the new IHR, the World Health Organisation has the power to act on information received from non-government sources, reducing the potential impact of non-compliance by States with their notification requirements (ibid.). States fail to comply with the IHR because of the threat to trade and tourism from disease outbreaks. To address this problem, the WHO may need to develop incentives to encourage compliance by States (Isasi and Nguyen 2005: 509).

The recent experience with the SARS crisis may be cause for cautious optimism. Although the IHR did not require notification of SARS, most countries with cases of SARS reported them voluntarily to WHO (Fidler 2004: 133). The new IHR also impose requirements on States that may be difficult for poorer countries to achieve, particularly when the public health systems of many poor countries are already struggling under the pressures of HIV/AIDS and the need to meet the requirements of the Millennium Development Goals (Fidler 2005: 391). The failure of the new IHR to address the issue of resource allocation, particularly for developing countries (Isasi and Nguyen 2005: 509), is a significant limitation in the scope of the IHR.

Rights in a Time of Crisis

An outbreak of pandemic disease will present legal and ethical challenges on an unprecedented scale. In the period since the 1918 influenza pandemic, our means of travel and communication have been transformed, making travel and communication with far distant places much easier. These changes are likely to facilitate the spread of disease, both globally and within countries, while international communications and the ability to be informed of disease outbreaks around the world, are likely to add to a growing sense of panic. In the period since 1918, our understandings of rights have also transformed. Western society has become increasingly focused on the individual, a trend evidenced by the primacy of the autonomy principle within contemporary bioethics. The rights-oriented nature of contemporary Western society is likely to pose challenges to attempts to formulate public health responses that seek to adopt a more communitarian outlook. Finally, as discussed above, the reconceptualization of public health ethics into an ethic premised on the continuity between public health and human rights demands the formulation of emergency responses that are consistent with human rights objectives. The task for public health law and ethics then is to formulate frameworks for decision-making in times of public health crises that reflect these contemporary understandings of rights.

Our responses to pandemic influenza will include both pharmaceutical and non-pharmaceutical measures. Unfortunately, in an influenza pandemic, pharmaceutical interventions (such as vaccines and antiviral medicines) will not be available to large numbers of the world's population. In the early stages of an outbreak of pandemic influenza, it is unlikely that an effective vaccine will be available (Booy et al. 2006). During this period, the use of existing antiviral drugs will be important in the fight against the disease (Department of Health and Ageing 2005: 107). However, no country has adequate stockpiles of antiviral drugs sufficient to treat their entire population, leading to calls for the utilization of non-voluntary licensing provisions under patent laws as a means of meeting the demand for antivirals (Davies 2006), and discussion of resource allocation during times of crisis (Gostin 2006).

In this context, non-pharmaceutical measures are likely to be of particular importance (World Health Organisation Writing Group, 2006a: 81). Non-pharmaceutical interventions are focused on limiting the potential for person-to-person spread of disease and include measures such as travel restrictions and screening of passengers to prevent international spread of disease; isolation, monitoring and quarantine; measures for social distancing such as closure of schools; reducing individual risk through the use of appropriate hygiene measures; and community education (ibid.: 81). During the 1918 flu pandemic, some island countries, including Australia, introduced maritime quarantine in an effort to prevent the introduction of influenza to their shores. As a result of these measures, the entry of the disease into Australia was delayed by about three months. (ibid.: 83–4). Non-pharmaceutical measures were also used during the SARS crisis in 2003. Screening for fevers at borders was used in an attempt to limit the spread of SARS but had limited effectiveness: 'data from 4 Asian locations and Canada indicated that body temperature-sensing devices did not detect anyone with SARS among >35 million entering travelers screened' (ibid.: 84). The World Health Organisation has recommended the use of exit screening of travellers, but acknowledges that screening is unlikely to be totally effective as it may miss asymptomatic travellers: 'As was true for SARS, the principal focus of WHO-recommended nonpharmaceutical interventions is not at international borders but at national and community levels' (ibid.: 86).

At the community level, reports from the 1918 flu pandemic suggest that mandatory case reporting and isolation of patients were ineffective in limiting the spread of influenza (World Health Organisation Writing Group 2006b: 88–9). Requesting affected individuals to remain at home is likely to be more effective and less socially disruptive but may require support for those affected (ibid.: 92). Depending on the means of transmission, the groups most affected and the severity of the disease, measures to increase social distance may be useful, and other public health measures such as handwashing and cough etiquette should be encouraged (ibid.: 92; Collignon and Carnie 2006). Although quarantine is an age-old public health tool (Gensini, Yacoub and Conti 2004), it has been noted that we need research 'to identify ways to make quarantine and other restrictions more focused and less burdensome for individual persons and societies and to assess how "leaky" restrictions can be and still be effective' (World Health Organisation Writing Group 2006b: 93).

During the SARS crisis, quarantine was used extensively in affected countries. In Toronto, health professionals accounted for more than 40 per cent of SARS cases and quarantine was imposed on many health professionals (Ries 2005: 538). The quarantine of health professionals and restricted access to hospitals at the height of the crisis created a backlog in the hospital system that had to be addressed after the crisis had passed (ibid.: 540). A Canadian report on the SARS crisis estimated that the direct cost of deferred surgical activity arising from SARS was $32.1 million (National Advisory Committee on SARS and Public Health 2003: 160). Quarantine also has the potential to have a negative economic impact on quarantined individuals. It has been noted that in Toronto 'Thousands of employees lost income while they stayed at home to observe quarantine or provide care for others who were quarantined...Some people had to use vacation time or take unpaid leave in order to observe quarantine' (Ries 2005: 540–41).

The psychosocial impacts of a crisis should not be underestimated. A Canadian report on SARS noted that the impact of SARS on people working in the health system included:

- people afraid to go to work in hospitals;
- people afraid to care for SARS patients;
- people afraid to associate with health care workers, or even spouses of health care workers, particularly those from SARS units;
- lingering resentment of colleagues who might not have contributed what was expected;
- people feeling helpless, angry, and guilty; and
- people experiencing acute social isolation and ostracism. [National Advisory Committee on SARS and Public Health 2003: 155]

Despite the risks posed by SARS, health professionals did not abandon their posts during the SARS crisis. However, infectious diseases may raise complex ethical questions about the duty of individual health professionals to act in times of crisis and about the risks that we as a society should expect them to bear (Reid 2005).

Part of the difficulty in formulating responses to public health crises is that certainty cannot be assumed. For example, if the public health emergency is precipitated by an outbreak of a new infectious disease (as occurred in 2003 with SARS), or an outbreak of a new strain of a known disease (as could occur in an outbreak of a new influenza strain), the severity of the disease and its path may be unknown during the initial stages of the outbreak. Gostin, Bayer and Fairchild have argued that public health ethics should be premised on the precautionary principle, a principle originally used in the context of evaluating responses to environmental hazards: 'The principle stipulates an obligation to protect populations against reasonably foreseeable threats, even under conditions of uncertainty' (2003: 3232; see also, Bayer and Fairchild 2004: 490). Gostin has argued that when acting to safeguard the health of the public the actions of public health authorities should be guided by a number of ethical values: transparency of decision-making; protection of vulnerable persons; fair treatment and social justice, including procedural justice and due process for individuals burdened by public health actions, and the utilization of the least restrictive alternative necessary to respond to the threat to health (Gostin 2004: 571–2). The articulation of these ethical values and principles is a vital part of developing an effective regulatory framework for public health emergencies.

In the United States, the Center for Law and the Public's Health at Georgetown and Johns Hopkins Universities drafted the Model State Emergency Health Powers Act (the Model Act).[3] The Model Act's purpose 'is to facilitate the detection, management, and containment of public health emergencies while appropriately safeguarding personal and proprietary interests' (Gostin et al. 2002: 625; see also, Erickson et al. 2002). The Act contains provisions relating to preparedness for public health emergencies, declaration of a state of public health emergency, special powers relating to management of property and protection of individuals during a state of public health emergency, and the dissemination of information to the public during the emergency. The inclusion of compulsory powers in the Model Act has been criticized for its restrictions on civil liberties (Annas 2002). Yet even in contemporary, individualistic society, individual rights are never absolute and are always bounded by the constraints of societal norms, rules, interests and relationships. The task of determining how to transcend the apparent tensions between the community and the individual remains a complex one. Ultimately, our ethical and legal principles must be guided by an understanding that public health is not simply about individuals but about the relationships between them (Childress and Bernheim 2003).

Feminist ideals of relational autonomy (discussed further in Chapter 7), also acknowledge the importance of social and family contexts and relationships in the formation of autonomous decisions. In short, relational autonomy recognizes that the decisions and actions of individuals are mediated by broader social and familial connections and that social relations are often marked by inequalities. This has implications for the ways we think about the relationships that characterize public health. As Wendy Rogers argues (2006: 354): 'In analysing the common good, feminists pay careful attention to such factors as: the criteria for community

3 The Model Act is available from the Center for Law and the Public's Health at <www.publichealthlaw.net>.

membership; the power relations that constitute the community; the rules that regulate it; where the benefits of community membership fall, and who pays the price for these.'

When public health is conceptualized with relationships at the core, the dichotomy between the individual and the community is no longer as stark. By starting with a focus on relationships, public health is no longer about either individuals or communities but rather about the ways in which they are mutually constitutive and the complementary, intersecting and overlapping rights and duties that arise in the shared space of contemporary society. It allows us to articulate public health goals in ways that respect the humanity and interests of individuals within a broader communal context.

Leslie Francis et al. argue that infectious diseases pose a challenge to understandings of autonomous agency in bioethics by requiring that agency is conceptualized in terms that are both embodied and relational: 'Contagious patients are not just ill by themselves; they are ill because of something that has come from others and could go to others' (2005: 321). Conceptualized in this way, infectious diseases raise new questions for our consideration that transcend a focus on individual rights:

> Is it a violation of agency, if the patient who has him/herself been a victim is required to consider how s/he might victimize others? Or if the ability of patients to enter clinical studies depends on both their own choices and the involvement of others to whom they might pose risks? Or consider justice, where providing a decent minimum of care world-wide may be critical to reducing everyone's vulnerability to disease? [ibid.]

The articulation of a relational and embodied ethics of public health does provide us with an opportunity to craft laws for public health emergencies and biopreparedness that recognize the importance of relationships in public health. Importantly, it will also provide an ethical framework for resolving and transcending apparent tensions between individual and community rights and interests that may arise in times of crisis, such as an outbreak of pandemic disease. In this sense then, a relational theory of public health ethics can provide a framework for the development of laws and policies at the national, state and local level. Furthermore, the articulation of ethical values for public health law, such as those identified by Gostin (2004) – transparency in decision-making, protection of the vulnerable, fair treatment and social justice, and the use of the least restrictive alternative – provides a foundation for regulatory development that is based on an appreciation of the link between the individual and the communal, and the relational context within which public health law operates.

As this chapter has argued, public health also needs to be understood in global terms and our theory of ethics must be adequate to the task of responding to concerns at the global level as well. The disproportionate burden of disease, including infectious disease, on the developing world, the huge disparities in global health and wealth, and the disproportionate access to medicines, demands that a relational theory of public health ethics also encompasses the global community and global relations and an effective framework for global health governance (Gostin 2007). This globalized understanding of public health law and ethics would focus on global efforts to ensure that the survival needs of the world's poor are met (Gostin 2007), through the provision of assistance for capacity-building of public health systems in developing countries, improved access to essential medicines, global cooperation in responding to infectious diseases including the 'neglected diseases' of the developing world, and the development of international relations designed to facilitate openness and transparency in the face of new disease threats. Much of this work is already under way through the work of various international agencies. Much work remains to be done.

The next outbreak of pandemic disease will provide a practical test of our understandings of ethics. In the period before a pandemic, there is an opportunity to develop our preparedness and to reflect upon the principles and values that will help to guide us through the crisis period. The next pandemic will test our compassion and our humanitarianism, both within our own local communities and more globally. In this period before the storm, we should articulate the values that we hold dear and ensure that our laws are crafted in ways that will ensure their protection.

Chapter 7

Autonomous Bodies

The issue of individual rights has been a fairly constant theme through the previous chapters as we have explored rights of access to assisted reproductive technology (ART), rights to knowledge of biological parentage, genetic rights, the rights of parents to choose the characteristics of their children, health rights and health tourism, and the rights of individuals and communities in times of pandemic influenza. The concept of individual autonomy is a close partner of individual rights for, in contemporary society, the autonomous individual is one separated from others in society by 'a wall (of rights)' (Nedelsky 1989: 12). Autonomy is a core concept in Western society. Drawing upon liberalism's ideal of the self-owning individual, autonomy has come to represent the ideal of the self-determining individual who has ownership of his or her own body. The autonomous individual is also very much an economic individual who is either financially self-sufficient or free to contract for his labour in the market-place.

Given the centrality of autonomy to the Western liberal tradition, it is hardly surprising then that autonomy has also taken a leading position within Western bioethical theory. It has become a core principle in health-care decision-making and increasingly has become the primary principle within principle-based ethics against which other principles such as beneficence, must be weighed. Health law too has reflected this preoccupation with autonomy – primarily through the articulation of principles relating to informed consent, rights of refusal of medical treatment and legal acknowledgement of patients' rights. This chapter explores the contemporary debates about the autonomous body to reveal the ways that autonomy is constructed within contemporary health law and ethics and the limits of those constructions.

Autonomy in Health Law

Within theories of principle-based ethics, autonomy has been one of four core principles: autonomy, beneficence, non-maleficence, and justice (Beauchamp and Childress 1989). While each of these principles is supposed to be of equal weight, as a practical matter the principle of autonomy has increasingly trumped other considerations. The social focus on the individual, combined with the growing recognition of patients' rights within health law and bioethics, has resulted almost in a preoccupation with autonomy and a withering of the consideration of other principles. The law also recognized autonomy in a wide variety of contexts and has upheld autonomy as a principle (Jackson 2000: 472). While greater attention to race- and gender-specific work has challenged principle-based ethics (Wolf 1994), autonomy has still managed to occupy a central place in health law and bioethics.

Two of the clearest expressions of health law's recognition and protection of bodily autonomy can be found in the law's treatment of the requirements relating to consent to medical treatment and in the duty of medical practitioners to disclose material risks of treatment to patients.

Consent is essential to autonomy. By deciding whether or not to undergo a particular form of medical treatment or health care, a patient is exercising their right of autonomous decision-making. For this reason, obtaining a patient's consent to treatment is integral to respect for a patient's autonomy. Consent is also an important precondition to medical treatment for legal reasons, as treatment that is performed without a valid consent may be unlawful. This concept derives from the protection of bodily integrity in both criminal and civil law. Within criminal law, it is an assault to use force, either intentionally or recklessly, on another person's body or clothing (McSherry and Naylor 2004: 159). Within tort law, any unauthorized contact with another's body could be regarded as a battery and therefore actionable. That battery is actionable *per se*, that is, without proof of damage, only serves to reinforce the role of law in protecting individuals from unwanted bodily contact. Of course, not all bodily contact is regarded as actionable. Some exceptions must exist in order for society to function. The law has recognized, for example, that exceptions may exist for 'the exigencies of everyday life' when people are jostled in busy streets or on public transport.[1] Furthermore, some forms of bodily contact may be prohibited by law. Consent does not make murder lawful.[2] In general however, the law does recognize the right of an individual to protection from unwanted bodily contact and provides legal remedies where that right is infringed.

The role of consent in contemporary health law is an extension of these general principles. As Australia's High Court has noted, 'Medical treatment of adults with full mental capacity does not come within any of the exceptions mentioned. The factor necessary to render such treatment lawful when it would otherwise be an assault is, therefore, consent.'[3] For health professionals, treatment carried out without the consent of the patient or an authorized decision-maker may expose the professional to legal liability for a trespass to the person. In order to provide protection against an action for trespass, a patient must have been advised in broad terms of the nature of the procedure and consented to it.[4] Of course, the patient may not always be able to provide consent for him or herself. Individuals may lack the capacity to consent because of age, illness, or disability. Children are generally regarded as unable to consent to medical treatment, and parental consent is usually exercised on behalf of the child. However, the right of a parent to consent to medical treatment of their minor child is, in Australia and Britain, regarded as dwindling as the young person gains maturity and capacity.[5]

1 *Collins v. Wilcock* [1984] 1 WLR 1172 at 1177.

2 *Secretary, Department of Health and Community Services v. JWB and SMB (Marion's Case)* [1991–92] 175 CLR 218 at 233, Mason CJ, Dawson, Toohey and Gaudron JJ.

3 *Secretary, Department of Health and Community Services v. JWB and SMB (Marion's Case)* [1991–92] 175 CLR 218 at 234, Mason CJ, Dawson, Toohey and Gaudron JJ.

4 *Chatterton v. Gerson* [1981] 1 QB 432 at 443; *Rogers v. Whitaker* [1992] 175 CLR 479 at 490.

5 *Gillick v. West Norfolk and Wisbech Area Health Authority* [1986] AC 112; *Secretary, Department of Health and Community Services v. JWB and SMB (Marion's Case)* [1991–92]

The respect for autonomy receives further recognition in the legal duty of doctors to provide patients with information about the material risks of treatment. The High Court of Australia has held that a risk is material if a reasonable person in the patient's position would be likely to attach significance to it or if the doctor is aware, or should be aware, that the particular patient would be likely to attach significance to the risk.[6] The High Court of Australia has commented:

> except in cases of emergency or necessity, all medical treatment is preceded by the patient's choice to undergo it. In legal terms, the patient's consent to the treatment may be valid once he or she is informed in broad terms of the nature of the procedure which is intended. But the choice is, in reality, meaningless unless it is made on the basis of relevant information and advice.[7]

Although this duty to advise on risks is usually referred to as 'informed consent', the High Court of Australia has noted that 'informed consent' is a term which 'is apt to mislead as it suggests a test of the validity of a patient's consent'.[8]

Owning the Body

The idea of autonomy as self-ownership raises the question of the extent to which individuals do actually have rights of ownership in relation to their bodies. As a general rule, there is no legal right to property in the human body or human tissue that has been excised from the body. But of course the idea that there can be no property in the body is only a partial story. The history of slavery reveals very clearly that bodies have been regarded as property (Hyde 1997: 95; Williams 1991). Furthermore, as Alan Hyde argues, the body must be able to be constructed as property in order for us to be able to sell our labour in the workforce (Hyde 1997: 50). Simultaneously though, through the construction of the autonomous self, the body is constructed as not property (ibid.: 57) and to attempt to do so appears to hearken back to the era of the slave trade. So while an individual can sell his or her labour in the market-place as one might sell any other form of property, the body is simultaneously marked out as something separate from the economic imperatives of property and the market: 'The body that cannot be property...thus marks the boundaries of an aesthetic realm that defines the boundaries of, and supplements, market society' (ibid.: 57).

In the 1908 case of *Doodeward v. Spence*,[9] the High Court of Australia considered whether a corpse could be property. Prior to the decision in *Doodeward*, a line of English cases had decided that there was no property in a human corpse, but that an individual could have a right to possession of a corpse, for example to ensure a proper burial for the body (Croucher 2006; Magnusson 1998: 27–37). In *Doodeward*, the plaintiff brought an action for detinue after a bottle containing the corpse of

175 CLR 218. For discussion of the issues relating to minors and medical treatment see New South Wales Law Reform Commission (2004).

6 *Rogers v. Whitaker* [1992] 175 CLR 479 at 490.

7 Ibid. at 489.

8 Ibid. at 490.

9 *Doodeward v. Spence* (1908) 6 CLR 406.

a stillborn two-headed child which the plaintiff had been exhibiting publicly was seized by the police and subsequently retained at a university museum. Griffith CJ held that a person could have a right of possession in a body or body part where the use of skill had changed the body into something different from a body before burial. In Griffith CJ's words:

> I entertain no doubt that, when a person has by the lawful exercise of work or skill so dealt with a human body or part of a human body in his lawful possession that it has acquired some attributes differentiating it from a mere corpse awaiting burial, he acquires a right to retain possession of it, at least as against any person not entitled to have it delivered to him for the purposes of burial, but subject, of course, to any positive law which forbids its retention under the particular circumstances.[10]

Barton J agreed with the judgment of Griffith CJ but stated his support for the principle that there was no property in an unburied corpse.[11] In his dissenting judgment, Higgins J rejected the idea that there could be property in a corpse and followed the line of cases which held that a corpse could not be property.[12]

Subsequent cases have upheld the principle that there can be no property in a corpse awaiting burial, although the administrators or executors of the deceased's estate may have a right of possession of the body to ensure its proper burial.[13] However, the idea that property interests may be possible in body parts or tissue that had been altered by the exercise of work or skill remains. Furthermore, case law has recognized that body parts are capable of becoming property and could, for example, be stolen.[14] Although an individual might be able to assert a proprietary interest in a tissue sample that has been altered by work or skill, excised tissue is not generally regarded as the property of the tissue provider (Magnusson 1998: 41–5). In the landmark United States case of *Moore v. the Regents of the University of California*,[15] the Supreme Court of California dismissed a claim by Moore for conversion in relation to the use of Moore's cells for research. The debate over whether individuals should be able to sell their organs, such as kidneys (Goodwin 2006; Griggs 1994; Wilkinson 2003), also serves to blur even further the property/not-property debate in relation to the body and its parts.

Increasingly, debate in this area has focused on the issue of 'benefit sharing' and the question of whether research participants have rights to share in the commercial benefits of research (Australian Law Reform Commission (ALRC) 2004: para. 3.48–3.55). While it has traditionally been argued that property rights could not be held over the human body, the debates about ownership of the body are beginning to be rewritten in the context of modern biotechnological research. Instead of regarding tissue samples as 'gifts' from research subjects to researchers, or relying on the idea that an individual has no legal interest in tissue once it has been excised from the

---

10 Ibid. at 414.

11 Ibid. at 417.

12 Ibid. at 421–2.

13 *Dobson v. North Tyneside Health Authority* [1997] 1 WLR 596 (CA).

14 *R v. Kelly* [1998] 3 All ER 741.

15 793 P 2d 479 (1990).

body, the commercialized nature of much modern research tends to lend weight to the idea of recognizing the interests that individuals have in their tissue samples through recognition of property rights (Knowles 1999). As Graeme Laurie has argued:

> A personal property paradigm could, in fact, serve an all-important role in completing the picture of adequate protection for the personality in tandem with other protectors such as autonomy, confidentiality and privacy. However, the added value of a property model lies in its ability to empower individuals and communities and to provide the crucial continuing control over samples or information through which ongoing moral and legal influence may be exerted. [2002: 316]

In its 2003 report on genetic privacy, the Australian Law Reform Commission articulated a number of advantages and disadvantages to applying a property model to human tissue. The advantages included:

- that an individual with property rights could assert that right against others;
- it would provide a mechanism for ongoing control of the sample;
- property rights encourage good record-keeping and the consensual use of samples;
- '[p]roperty rights clarify the gift relationship between donors and researchers by defining which rights over the sample may be transferred, when and how';
- an individual whose rights have been violated has access to legal remedies;
- property rights can be transferred to others, and
- property rights provide a mechanism for benefit-sharing from the profits of research. [2003: para. 20.20]

The disadvantages with applying a property model to genetic samples include:

- a property model might be seen as permitting the commodification of the human body;
- it may affect the willingness of individuals to donate their tissue freely;
- tissue sales would result in increased costs to researchers and ultimately consumers;
- legal actions might be able to be brought against those who deal with tissue samples that have been inadvertently discarded, even if the sample is not being misused;
- an individual who transfers rights in their tissue to someone else could lose their interest in preventing uses of the tissue that he or she objects to;
- a property rights model could undermine the current system for ethical oversight of research by Human Research Ethics Committees which allows the requirement for consent to be waived in certain circumstances, and
- it is difficult to apply property rights 'to genetic material, which can be copied and reproduced.' [2003: para. 20.21]

The Commission ultimately rejected the use of a property model as a means of protecting genetic information:

> However, the Inquiry has come to the view that the drawbacks of a property approach are considerable and outweigh the potential benefits at the present time. The recognition of property rights in human tissue has developed slowly in a piecemeal fashion under the common law, as new situations have been brought before the courts. As several submissions noted, there may be unforeseen consequences of extending property law to cover genetic samples, due largely to the strength of the rights that property law provides. As a result, property law may be a rather 'blunt instrument' for protecting a person's interest in his or her genetic samples. [2003: para. 20.34]

Enclosing the Body

The new genetics has highlighted a range of issues about the commercialization of biotechnology and with it issues relating to control over tissue samples. The increasing commercialization of biomedical research has sparked concerns over the ethics of patenting human genes, and the ethics of exploiting gene patents (ALRC 2004: para. 3.36–3.65). The debates about commercialization of research and property rights in the human body and tissue are essentially debates about the ethics of privatizing things that have traditionally been regarded either as not capable of being owned, or if they were, as having common ownership, that is, as being in the public domain. Debates over the ethics of patenting human genes are at the heart of this contemporary debate.

Of course, this is not the first time that we have seen the expansion of property rights and concepts to things once thought to have public ownership. In feudal times, the commons was the common land owned and used communally. The transformations in property systems which allowed for the 'enclosure' of common lands and their passage from common to private ownership is known as the enclosure movement (Boyle 2003: 33–4). The tragedy of the commons is that it did not encourage the maximum productive use of the land. There were no incentives to improve the land or the systems for its use and it is undoubtedly the case that the enclosure of common lands unleashed considerable productive potential. However, the enclosure movement also had a dark side, disrupting established social patterns and communities, and divesting the poorer classes of their interests in the land (ibid.: 35). Boyle has described the current extension of intellectual property rights as 'the second enclosure movement': 'True, the new state-created property rights may be "intellectual" rather than "real," but once again things that were formerly thought of as either common property or uncommodifiable are being covered with new, or newly extended, property rights' (ibid.: 37). While referring to the extension of patent rights over human genes as an example of this contemporary enclosure, Boyle points out that other areas are also increasingly being enclosed. As he points out, 'Patents are increasingly stretched out to cover "ideas" that twenty years ago all scholars would have agreed were unpatentable' (ibid.: 39).

This extension of private property rights is occurring despite the public investment in health and biotechnology research. In Australia, most health-related biotechnology research is publicly funded and is carried out in universities, research institutions and organizations, and health departments (ALRC 2004: para. 11.2). In 2001, the expenditure of public funds for biotechnology research amounted to approximately A$300 million (ibid.: para. 11.10). While a great deal of biotechnology research takes place in the public sector, the question of how to maximize public benefit from biotechnology research has become an important issue (ibid.: para. 11.15), since the 'privatization' of research results in the form of patents, is a key aspect of the commercialization process: 'Patenting is vital to the pharmaceutical and medical biotechnology industries because of the costs and long lead time between the discovery of a new drug, diagnostic or therapy and the acquisition of marketing approval (estimated to take around 12 years for most pharmaceuticals)' (Nichol and Nielsen 2001: 348).

Although intellectual property and patent rights are supposed to facilitate and encourage research and the building of research capacity, the existence of intellectual property law can also complicate the commercialization process and make it more expensive. There is the potential for patents to stifle research rather than facilitate it. The existence of multiple upstream patents, known as 'patent thickets', provides a complex array of intellectual property rights that must be negotiated in order to commercialize new technology (ALRC 2004: para. 18.12). Furthermore, 'royalty stacking', the requirement for payment of multiple licence fees, can increase prices and discourage the development of new products (ibid.: para. 18.19). Heller and Eisenberg have described the multiplication of biomedical patents as 'the tragedy of the anticommons' (1998: 698). In this situation, 'multiple owners each have a right to exclude others from a scarce resource and no one has an effective privilege of use' (ibid.). When an anticommons develops, biomedical innovation is stifled:

> The tragedy of the anticommons refers to the more complex obstacles that arise when a user needs access to multiple patented inputs to create a single useful product. Each upstream patent allows its owner to set up another tollbooth on the road to product development, adding to the cost and slowing the pace of downstream biomedical innovation. [ibid.: 699]

Indeed, it seems that somewhat paradoxically the second enclosure movement described by Boyle, a form of contemporary anticommons, has created a situation where we see the development of 'the tragedy of the anticommons' described by Heller and Eisenberg. Rather than unlocking productive potential, the complexity and expansion of private rights through the contemporary patent system has the potential to add new barriers to research and development.

Gametes and Embryos

The consistent denial of recognition of property rights in relation to excised human tissue can be contrasted with the debates over treatment of gametes and embryos that are outside the body. Although there has been disquiet about utilizing a property-based model for gametes and embryos used in assisted reproductive technology (ART), this has been coupled with a need to provide a mechanism for articulating the interests that individuals and couples have in their reproductive material. Thus the concern to articulate the nature of the legal interests that individuals have in their extra-corporeal gametes and embryos contrasts sharply with the rejection of such interests in relation to other tissue.

In Australia in the mid-1980s, the Waller Committee in Victoria rejected the idea that a couple owned their stored ART embryo on the basis that these concepts 'have no place in a consideration of issues which focus on an individual and genetically unique human entity' (1984: para. 2.8). The Committee regarded the interests of a couple in their ART embryo as being 'analogous to those recognized in parents of a child after its birth' (ibid.). The Senate Select Committee on the Human Embryo Experimentation Bill 1985 also rejected a property model for human embryos, preferring instead a guardianship approach which would see the property interests of gamete donors as ending upon fertilization: 'At that point guardianship arises and would be ordinarily and properly exercised by the intending social parents (whether or not these are the same persons as the gamete donors)' (1986: para. 3.41).[16] Following the 'not property' approach, the Supreme Court of Tennessee decided in the case of *Davis v. Davis*[17] 'that preembryos are not, strictly speaking, either "persons" or "property", but occupy an interim category that entitles them to special respect because of their potential for human life.' Although not property, the Court held that the couple did have 'an interest in the nature of ownership, to the extent that they have decision-making authority concerning disposition of the preembryos within the scope of policy set by law.'[18]

In the United Kingdom, the Warnock Committee in its 1984 report recommended that the 'embryo of the human species be afforded some protection in law' (Warnock 1984: para. 11.17). This position was endorsed in 2005 by the House of Commons Science and Technology Committee report (2005: para. 28): 'While this gradualist approach to the status of the embryo may cause difficulties in the drafting of legislation, we believe that it represents the most ethically sound and pragmatic solution and one which permits in vitro fertilisation and embryo research within certain constraints set out in legislation.' The Committee was also of the view that human embryo research could be carried out without compromising the special status of the embryo but that there should be proper ethical oversight of the research (ibid.: para. 50).

As is clear from the above discussion, embryos have special significance because of their developmental potential and it is this potentiality that makes the language of property seem harsh and inappropriate when applied in the reproductive context. As Jennifer Nedelsky points out the concept of property does not adequately speak to the attachments we have in reproduction:

> The values at stake in the cases turn out to be about honouring and protecting the kind of attachment to potential life that is appropriate for fostering relations of respect and appreciation of children. I think the issues in the cases also touch the most general concern of fostering people's capacities to form relationships of intimacy, trust and responsibility. These issues involve allocation of control and decision-making authority, but they are not about ownership. [1993: 363]

The application of property concepts to gametes and embryos is inappropriate therefore because the language of property is inadequate for dealing with the potential

16 For discussion of this report, see Albury (1989); Kasimba and Buckle (1988; 1989).

17 842 SW 2d 588 at 597 (Tenn 1992).

18 Ibid.

relationships that are represented by the embryo. The significance of embryos, and to a lesser extent gametes, can only be understood in relational and embodied terms.

It is this link to potentiality that is so important in the debates about embryos. Although some regard an embryo as a person from the time of conception, official responses to assisted reproduction have tended to prefer an approach based on providing respect for the embryo based on its potential to develop into a person. What is intriguing about the potentiality argument is the complex nature of the link to embodiment that is evident within these debates. It is the potentially embodied nature of embryonic development that is seen as providing the foundation for its special treatment and the inappropriateness of property concepts. Yet arguably in the case of embryos created for research or even those donated for research, the link to embodiment in terms of realization of embryonic potential has been disconnected or never existed in the first place (Karpin 2006). These are embryos that will never be implanted into a woman's body and thus will never have the potential to develop into a person. Of course, the link to embodiment still remains on one level as gametes are vital if stem cell research is to occur and, given the greater difficulties in obtaining ova rather than sperm, women make a significant contribution to stem cell research. Yet, as Donna Dickenson argues, 'In most commentaries and debates, the women from whom the ova are taken have virtually disappeared from view' (2006: 43). The embodied nature of embryos tends to be glossed over in the debates over embryo research in which all embryos are regarded as morally equal even while distinctions are drawn between them as to the uses to which they may be put. As Isabel Karpin has argued:

> The embryo is only connected with its potential for personhood by female embodiment. Those who wish to make the argument that all embryos have equivalent value do so only by rendering the female body irrelevant. In order to do this, a complex process of disappearing has to take place. If we return the female body to visibility then the basis of the discussion is fundamentally changed. [2006: 603]

As Karpin argues, within the debates over human embryo research it is the embryo, disconnected from its embodied links with a woman, that occupies the central place in debates over legislative reform.

In a further twist on the embodiment aspect of the stem cell debates, the arguments in favour of special protection for the embryo resonate with more traditional debates against abortion (Dolgin 2003). Yet, as Janet Dolgin argues, in the stem cell debates we do not see the arguments of protection of the embryo/foetus versus the woman's rights of autonomy and choice, that are so familiar to us from the abortion context. Rather, as Dolgin points out:

> ...autonomous choice is assumed and claims about embryonic personhood are countered by claims about cures for sick children, dying adults, and people suffering from an array of serious, debilitating conditions. Such claims are compelling in a society committed to the notion that health brings salvation. The mode of cure suggested by embryonic stem cell therapy – a uniquely *individual* form of therapy – provides a metaphor for a society increasingly committed to autonomous individuality. [2003: 146]

Dolgin argues that the focus on the embryo in the context of debates over cloning and stem cell research is reconfiguring the debate over abortion against a backdrop that takes autonomy and choice for granted (ibid.: 154). The legal debate that occurs around the status and disposition of spare ART embryos 'reflects a society often ready to define embryos instrumentally but anxious at the same time to mask that fact from itself' (ibid.: 156). While the abortion debate conceptualized embryos as mini-people, the stem cell debate allows for a reimagining in which embryos are regarded as cells that have significance because of their potential to cure disease (ibid.: 157).

Within official reports, there are some signs of recognition of the importance of the link to embodiment and of the need to draw distinctions *between* embryos. In the United Kingdom, the House of Commons Science and Technology Committee report noted the difficulties in defining the embryo at a time of rapidly changing science stating that 'The attempt to define an embryo in the HFE [Human Fertilisation and Embryology] Act has proved counter-productive' (2005: para. 53). The Committee recommended an alternative approach:

> We consider that a better approach would be to define the forms of embryo that can be implanted and under what circumstances. Using this approach, only those forms of embryo specified by the legislation, such as those created by fertilisation, could be implanted in the womb and thereby used for reproductive purposes. Other forms of embryo would be regulated insofar as they are created and used for research purposes. [ibid.]

In Australia, the Lockhart Review recommended that the creation of embryos by nuclear transfer for research be permitted under licence[19] and provided five reasons in support of this approach:

- While reproductive cloning aims to copy a person, SCNT [somatic cell nuclear transfer] only aims to copy a person's cells; therefore, provided the person consents, there is no objection to this.
- In addition, if the embryo created by SCNT is not intended to be implanted, it does not represent a potential new individual in the way that the product of fertilisation does.
- After nuclear transfer, the new cell needs to develop to the blastocyst stage so the inner cell mass can be removed, and while this entity is indistinguishable from other types of human embryos, it has been created specifically for research purposes (which is currently prohibited under the PHC [Prohibition of Human Cloning] Act).
- However, this type of embryo is not intended to be implanted, so the production and destruction of such an embryo is not dissimilar to the production and destruction of excess ART embryos, which is permitted by the legislation and accepted by society.
- Therefore, if research on excess ART embryos is permitted, it is not a major additional step to permit SCNT. [2005: 171]

Within both of these reports, we can see the link to implantation (that is, embodiment) being used as a means of drawing distinctions between embryos – some of which are

19 Many of the recommendations of the Lockhart Review have now been adopted in legislation following the Prohibition of Human Cloning for Reproduction and the Regulation of Human Embryo Research Amendment Act 2006 (Cth). For further discussion see Chapter 3.

destined for implantation and others that are destined for research and that will never be implanted (Karpin 2006). Despite the new focus on implantation, embryos rather than the women who might carry them, still occupy the primary place in the debates over embryo research, with implantation becoming a means of choosing between embryos in terms of deciding which regulatory framework applies to them.

The Relational Body

In some respects, the dissociation between embryos and women's bodies should hardly be surprising. Reproduction and reproductive relationships have long proven to be thorny issues for legal analysis. To a significant degree, this is because liberal legalism is premised on individualistic and atomistic conceptualizations of autonomy that prove inadequate for the task of speaking to the connected nature of women's lives.

The relationship of pregnancy does not fit easily into the liberal conceptualizations of individuality and separateness. The interconnected nature of the maternal/foetal relationship is a unique bodily experience. While pregnancy is about connectedness, the language of rights and autonomy is about separation. Women have long argued for the right to autonomous decision-making in the context of reproductive decision-making. Indeed, the feminist slogan of 'a woman's right to choose' about whether to continue with a particular pregnancy is a clear appeal to the language of autonomy and rights. However, as Carl Stychin points out, the reliance of feminists on autonomy and self-ownership is increasingly problematic because reproduction by women is increasingly a focus of legal and medical discourses and state regulation (1998: 223).

Technology has undoubtedly recast the debates about the foetus. Technologies such as ultrasound, which allow us to view the developing foetus, and the ability to perform *in utero* foetal surgery have contributed to the characterization of the foetus as a separate patient during pregnancy and as an autonomous being that is somehow separate and distinct from the pregnant woman. As Isabel Karpin has pointed out, with the growing knowledge about the ways that a pregnant woman can impact upon her foetus, 'the response of law and science has been to see these connections as a point of competition between mother and foetus and as a mark of their separate trajectories' (1992: 330). A link with disability is also significant for, as Rothschild points out, 'As the defective fetus becomes the focus of medical attention, the pregnant woman is eclipsed as primary patient' (2005: 214). Of course, actual disability is not a requirement here. The focus on the foetal patient directs medical attention not only to diagnosis of actual disability but also to protecting and ensuring the health of the foetus during the pregnancy so as to avoid actual disability. It is in this context that maternal behaviour during pregnancy acquires new significance in terms of its potential (deleterious) impact on the developing foetus.

The conceptualization of the foetus as a bearer of individual rights and interests draws a line around the foetal body in ways that mark the foetus as something separate from the pregnant body that nurtures it. Against this backdrop 'foetal rights' have been defined in ways that are oppositional to those of the pregnant woman. As

Nancy Rhoden has commented, 'The technology for treating the foetus as a patient within a patient has transformed the unity of pregnancy into an uneasy duality' (1987: 120). The abortion wars are clearly fought over the rights of women versus the rights of the foetus. These oppositional arguments have seeped through to the law and are evident in the debates over substance abuse and addiction during pregnancy and court-ordered caesarean sections (Anderson 2000; Rhoden 1987; Scott 2000). Within these debates is the argument that women have a moral duty to act in ways that ensure the well-being of the foetus and that the rights of the foetus have primacy over the rights of the pregnant woman during the pregnancy. In *Jefferson v. Griffin Spalding County Hospital Authority*,[20] the Superior Court authorized a caesarean section after the pregnant woman refused one on religious grounds. In reaching its decision the Court held that the intrusion into the parents' lives was outweighed by the State's duty to protect the life of the unborn child. The Supreme Court of Georgia denied the parents' motion for a stay.[21]

Judith Jarvis Thomson has challenged the argument of the moral duty owed by a pregnant woman in her famous analysis of duties to the unconscious violinist. Thomson asks us to imagine as follows:

> You wake up in the morning and find yourself back to back in bed with an unconscious violinist. A famous unconscious violinist. He has been found to have a fatal kidney ailment, and the Society of Music Lovers has canvassed all the available medical records and found that you alone have the blood type to help. They have therefore kidnapped you, and last night the violinist's circulatory system was plugged into yours, so that your kidneys can be used to extract poisons from his blood as well as your own. [1971: 48–9]

In Thomson's scenario, it is not possible for the violinist to be unplugged for nine months without ending his life. At the end of the nine-month period, the violinist will have recovered and can be safely unplugged (ibid.: 49). The ethical question that Thomson poses is whether you are morally obliged to remain connected to the unconscious violinist. For Thomson, the violinist's interest in life does not require you to volunteer the use of your body for nine months to support his life, nor does it justify the imposition of the obligation by a third party. To unplug the connection with the violinist would not be morally wrong. Thomson draws a distinction between the Minimally Decent Samaritan and the Good Samaritan. For Thomson, we should not fall below the standard of the Minimally Decent Samaritan which means that while abortion is not morally impermissible, neither is it always permissible (ibid.: 65). Furthermore, the right that exists is a right to bodily separation, not a right to ensure the death of the foetus (ibid.: 66).

In her work on abortion and embodiment, Catriona Mackenzie (1992) develops a feminist analysis of autonomous decision-making about abortion that moves beyond the traditional competing rights and bodily autonomy abortion arguments. Mackenzie puts forward four arguments for moving beyond these traditional understandings (ibid.: 137). First, she argues that the characterization of abortion decisions as being about conflicting rights between the pregnant woman and her foetus misrepresents

---

20 (1981) Ga 274 SE 2d 457.

21 Ibid. at 460. For discussion see Scott (2000: 11–12).

the relationship of pregnancy and the ways that a woman exercises her autonomy during pregnancy. Secondly, there is an oversimplification of our conceptualization of foetal status. Third, the focus on autonomy does not adequately take account of the embodied relationship of pregnancy and finally, abortion arguments based on the woman's right to bodily autonomy logically only grants a right to foetal evacuation and not foetal death.

Abortion decisions are not often seen as maternal decisions. Indeed, a decision to terminate a pregnancy is usually seen as exactly the opposite of a maternal, caring decision. Yet, relationships and caring are at the core of women's decision-making about abortion. As Leslie Cannold notes 'Women's decisions about abortion are the same sorts of decisions they make about mothering, only with different outcomes' (1998: xvi). Mackenzie argues that a feminist theory of abortion must incorporate the relational aspects of autonomous reproductive decision-making (1992: 138). Although a foetus does not have full moral rights, it can have moral significance through its relations with others who have decided 'to take parental responsibility for its future well-being' (ibid.: 143). In circumstances where a woman has decided to take parental responsibility for a foetus, her relationship to the foetus is similar to guardianship. This primary moral guardianship role cannot be assumed by a man during pregnancy because the foetus and woman are physically inseparable. Once the foetus has been born, any responsible adult can care for the foetus (ibid.). Mackenzie acknowledges that it is the potentiality of the foetus that gives it moral significance, with the complexity of foetal development being relevant to its potentiality. In other words, as the embryo and foetus develop and become more complex the potentiality of the foetus undergoes significant changes (ibid.: 145). It is precisely because of the embodied nature of the pregnancy relationship that self-determination issues are so central to abortion decisions: 'The experience of pregnant embodiment... affects a woman's mode of being-in-the-world both physically and morally and, as a consequence, reshapes her sense of self. She is no longer just herself but herself and another, but this other is not yet separate from herself' (ibid.: 151). It is this conceptualization of pregnancy as a complex mixing of bodily separation and connection, which Karpin refers to as 'not-one-but-not-two' (1992: 329), that makes it impossible to understand pregnancy within the traditional understandings of bodily separation.

In some landmark decisions, the courts have accepted the indivisibility of pregnancy and have asserted the validity of autonomous decision-making, making strong statements about the importance of protecting autonomy. In *Dobson (Litigation Guardian of) v. Dobson*,[22] the Supreme Court of Canada considered whether a woman's child could sue the woman for her driving during pregnancy which had allegedly injured the woman's child while in utero. The majority judgment rejected the analogy of the tort liability of a third party for prenatal injuries stating, 'a pregnant woman must stand in a uniquely different situation to her foetus than any third party.'[23] As the majority noted:

22 (1999) 174 DLR (4th) 1. For discussion see Scott (2000).

23 *Dobson* ibid. at para. 29.

> In contrast to the third-party defendant, a pregnant woman's every waking and sleeping moment, in essence, her entire existence, is connected to the foetus she may potentially harm. If a mother were to be held liable for prenatal negligence, this could render the most mundane decision taken in the course of her daily life as a pregnant woman subject to the scrutiny of the courts.[24]

In *Winnipeg Child and Family Services (Northwest Area) v. G(D.F.)*,[25] the Supreme Court of Canada confirmed a decision of the Manitoba Court of Appeal setting aside an order by a trial judge detaining a pregnant woman who was addicted to glue-sniffing. In the majority judgment, McLachlin J commented:

> the common law does not clothe the courts with power to order the detention of a pregnant woman for the purpose of preventing harm to her unborn child. Nor, given the magnitude of the changes and their potential ramifications, would it be appropriate for the courts to extend their power to make such an order. The changes to the law sought on this appeal are best left to the wisdom of the elected legislature.[26]

In the English case of *St George's Healthcare NHS Trust v. S; R v. Collins and Others, ex parte S*,[27] a woman (S) applied for judicial review of a court declaration which had dispensed with her consent to medical treatment and authorized treatment including a caesarean section. Following the declaration, S's child was delivered by caesarean section and S subsequently sought judicial review of the declaration. The Court of Appeal held that S should not have been detained under the mental health legislation and allowed S's appeal against the declaration. In delivering the judgment of the Court of Appeal, Judge LJ said:

> In our judgment while pregnancy increases the personal responsibilities of a woman it does not diminish her entitlement to decide whether or not to undergo medical treatment. Although human, and protected by the law in a number of different ways...an unborn child is not a separate person from its mother. Its need for medical assistance does not prevail over her rights. She is entitled not to be forced to submit to an invasion of her body against her will, whether her own life or that of her unborn child depends on it.[28]

The relationship of pregnancy is the obvious example of the relational body. The experience of conjoined twins may provide another example. Both situations highlight the inadequacies of existing ethical and legal understandings of autonomy. Certainly the debates around pregnancy reveal a problem which is both legal and ethical and which, as Rosamund Scott points out, 'lies at the interface between the subjective domain of rights and the objective arena of duties, both moral and legal' (2000: 4). In order to move beyond this dilemma we need to develop new language about rights, autonomy and embodiment.

---

24 Ibid. at para. 27.
25 (1997) 152 DLR (4th) 193. For discussion see Scott (2000).
26 *Winnipeg* ibid. at para. 59.
27 [1998] 3 All ER 673 (CA).
28 [1998] 3 All ER 673 at 692.

Relational Autonomy

The relational nature of pregnant embodiment and the inadequacy of theories of autonomy built on separation demanded alternative theories of autonomy. Furthermore, the fact that women (and their reproductive capacity) have often been seen as 'belonging' to men in their capacity as husbands and fathers has drained the concept of autonomy of much of its meaning for women. Ngaire Naffine argues that:

> The structure of self-ownership therefore, of necessity, applied only to the male body which was thought to be free from the encumbrances of sex and reproduction and yet which still depended on ready and exclusive access to the fertile body of a woman for its reproductive needs (both physical and economic). [1998: 204]

Liberalism, and the Cartesian split between body and mind, have tended to privilege those attributes traditionally associated with men and masculinity and marginalize those associated with women and femininity (Lacey 1998: 107–108). The equation of women with their bodies (embodiment), thus constructs women in opposition to mind and culture, with which men are equated (Stychin 1998: 215).

Martha Fineman has described autonomy as one of the 'foundational myths' of American society (2004: ch. 1). Along with the concepts of independence and self-sufficiency, autonomy is, according to Fineman, woven together in popular and political rhetoric about individuals and obligations in contemporary society. Yet despite the fact that the language of autonomy seems to be ever-present in contemporary discourse, 'there is no consensus about what the concept means or when it can be legitimately employed' (Mackenzie and Stoljar 2000: 4–5).

Feminist theories of the body have challenged the conceptualization of the male body as the generic body of society and have reconfigured the body as both embodied and social (Karpin 1992; Mykitiuk 1994; Naffine 1997; Stychin 1998). As Alan Hyde has argued (1997: 11): '*body autonomy* is an oxymoron. Bodies may indeed be experienced as autonomous, but, where this is so, this is because of their social, discursive construction as autonomous. Body autonomy is really social, public, and conventional.'

Rather than rejecting the concept of autonomy, feminist theories of autonomy thus seek to develop new understandings of autonomy (Mackenzie and Stoljar 2000: 3). Drawing upon feminist theories of 'caring' and connectedness, feminist theorists have posited alternative outlooks on society and social relations, suggesting a focus on caring rather than rights.[29] Known as 'relational autonomy', and covering a range of perspectives within feminist theory, they all share a common belief 'that persons are socially embedded and that agents' identities are formed within the context of social relationships and shaped by a complex of intersecting social determinants, such as race, class, gender, and ethnicity' (ibid.: 4). The challenge for feminists is, as Jennifer Nedelsky points out, one of 'how to combine the claim of

29 The work of Carol Gilligan has been enormously influential here. Gilligan's landmark work argued that men and women approach ethical dilemmas in different ways with men focusing on rights and women focusing on caring.

the constitutiveness of social relations with the value of self-determination' (1989: 9). Anne Donchin argues that a reformulation of autonomy requires 'a positive conception of human agency that recognizes relational experiences as an integral dimension of individuality' (2001: 367).

Drawing upon care-based ethics within feminist theory, Jennifer Nedelsky has argued for autonomy to be understood in terms of caring. Rejecting a property-based model for autonomy, Nedelsky argues instead for autonomy to be understood in related and interdependent ways with child-rearing replacing property as autonomy's symbol (1989: 12). For Nedelsky, 'relatedness is not, as our tradition teaches, the antithesis of autonomy, but a literal precondition of autonomy, and interdependence a constant component of autonomy' (ibid.). The eighteenth-century significance of private property as a symbolic marker of the boundary between government and individual independence is not longer applicable to life in modern society where the state increasingly licences and regulates activities: 'The task is to make the independence of citizen and state conducive to, rather than destructive of, autonomy' (ibid.: 20). Although property remains a powerful symbol of the freedom of the individual to act without state intervention, in fact, as Nedelsky points out, the power and authority of the state are essential to giving meaning to property rights (ibid.: 23).

Nedelsky argues that there is however, 'a basic truth' in the opposition of autonomy and collectivity. The problem with the tradition of equating autonomy with separation is that the oppositional nature of the relationship between the autonomous and the collective is highlighted, while the non-oppositional aspects of the relationship are underdeveloped (ibid.: 21). Nedelsky argues that we need to understand autonomy in more relational and nuanced ways: 'The collective is not simply a potential threat to individuals, but is constitutive of them, and thus is a source of their autonomy as well as a danger to it' (ibid.).

Leslie Bender also draws upon an ethic of caring in her reconceptualization of autonomy, arguing that 'In a care-based ethic, individual autonomy is a *process* nurtured in webs of relationships and responsibilities instead of a static condition pre-existing them' (1992: 536). For Bender, autonomy within a care-based ethics does not involve 'governing alone' but rather 'means choosing options with respect to responsibilities, relationships, conversations, and dialogues with others' (ibid.: 537). Understood in this way, Bender sees autonomous decision-making as being transformed from a concept based on individualized decision-making into an interactive, interdependent process built on relationships (ibid.). Bender argues that understanding autonomy in terms of care-based ethics will allow us to overcome some of the rights-based tensions that exist in debates about death and dying and instead allow us to understand that death is a process and that heroic interventions for dying patients may not always be the best means of caring for the patient (ibid.: 540).

Martha Fineman puts forward a theory of autonomy conceptualized in terms of dependency. She argues that by equating state provision of financial benefits with dependency, and therefore loss of autonomy, as occurs in contemporary American discourse, that the concept of autonomy as self-sufficiency 'is on a collision course with another important aspiration in the American constellation of political ideals – the promise of equality of opportunity and access to societal goods and services' (2004: 9). Fineman argues for a rethinking of autonomy which sees autonomy conceptualized in terms of the 'webs of economic and social relationships that sustain us' (ibid.: 28). Autonomy, for Fineman, is only realized through equality and social support. Thus, for Fineman, autonomy is only understood in terms that expressly appreciate the dependency of individuals within their social context.

Autonomy and Connectedness

As is clear from the discussion in this chapter, although autonomy has a central place in contemporary health law jurisprudence, the conceptualization of individuals as separate possessors of rights is challenged by the practical realities in which autonomy is exercised. Despite the rhetoric of self-ownership that attaches to autonomy, there has been a reluctance to recognize property rights in the body, although this too is increasingly complicated by the commercial aspects of contemporary health research and the ever-expanding nature of intellectual property. The reluctance to extend property rights to the body is also evident in debates about human embryos which have been regarded as needing special respect because of their potentiality in terms of human development. Paradoxically, although this respect only makes sense when embryos are considered in terms of embodiment, the potentiality argument is also evident in debates about embryos that are destined for research and that will never develop as individuals. Feminists have argued that the body must be understood in relational terms which see pregnancy as a relationship of shared interests rather than a source of conflict between a woman and her foetus. These arguments about embodiment link with development of theories of relational autonomy which seek to move beyond the limitations of autonomy understood in individualized terms and towards a deeper appreciation of the links that bind us all to each other. Autonomy is not simply about the rights and ability of an individual to assert his or her interests against the rest of the world. Rather, it is more nuanced, more relational. It is about the ways that our desires, dreams and interests may be expressed within the rich, complex and unruly tangle of relationships that are part of life in modern society. Without this understanding, autonomy remains just an empty shell.

Chapter 8

Health Law's Kaleidoscope: Concluding Thoughts

In the chapters of this book I have tried to show the possibilities – both positive and negative – that shape the landscape of contemporary health law, and the ways that the patterns of our lives intersect and overlap in a variety of unruly ways that present constant new challenges for law and ethics. Assisted reproductive technologies have reconfigured our lives, and our futures, by bringing together strangers through gamete donation in ways that are designed simultaneously to be both deeply personal (the creation of a child) and emotionally distant (donor anonymity). Our sense of certainty about the moral status of a human embryo has been cast adrift by scientific developments which allow us to choose whether an embryo should have the potential to develop into a child or whether the embryo should be used in more instrumental ways to develop stem cells that may, in turn, potentially offer new therapeutic possibilities for the treatment of illness and disease. Cloning technologies present their own set of challenges and, despite the widespread condemnation of cloning of whole humans through reproductive cloning, the question of whether a clone can have human dignity remains a complex and vexed question. While our children may still be gifts from nature, the ability to choose between gifts through preimplantation genetic diagnosis of embryos has added new ethical complexities to reproductive decision-making. While it is perhaps true that, far more than any generation before us, we hold the keys to humanity in our hands, through both genetic technologies and reproductive technologies, there is little consensus about which doors should be unlocked using those keys.

Life now is rarely predictable in the ways that it may have been in previous times and we are, as Giddens points out, now living in a society that is increasingly preoccupied with the future and the management of risk (1999: 3). The extensive nature of statutory protections and statutory authorities attests to the role that law plays in managing and responding to risk. Yet the management of risk is increasingly difficult. The globalized nature of economic and scientific progress runs up against the jurisdictionally based nature of law and legal regulation. In Chapter 5, I revealed how the joint phenomena of recognition of health rights and growing ease of international travel combine to present the new dilemmas of medical migration, fertility tourism and transplant tourism. In each of these areas, the economic poverty and aspirations of people in the world's poorer countries encounter the economic wealth and aspirations of people from the world's wealthy countries. To borrow from the work of Thomas Friedman (2005), this is where the flat world meets the unflat world. Risk is also evident in the concerns over pandemic influenza discussed in Chapter 6. Once again, flatness meets unflatness in the global disparities evident in the burden of disease and in the potential for infectious diseases to cross borders and have a global impact.

Rights and connection are constant themes in all these discussions. In Australia, as elsewhere, the language of rights is increasingly evident in health law debates. Autonomy walks side by side with rights, ensuring that rights are primarily articulated in highly individualized ways. Of course, the language of autonomy is not new. As Chapter 7 pointed out, our contemporary understandings of autonomy are built upon eighteenth-century concepts of self-ownership and freedom from state interference. Yet autonomy conceptualized in individualized terms is only one aspect of autonomy and fails to take account of the social setting for the lives of individuals. For most of us, autonomy is exercised in ways that are connected with and mediated through our relationships to others. Thus, as argued in Chapter 6, concepts of individual autonomy and agency may make little sense in terms of the management of communal risk from the spread of infectious diseases such as influenza. Instead, autonomy needs to be seen in ways that are connected to the community and communal responses need to take account of the needs of affected individuals.

Yet even if there are points of intersection in our lives, what can we learn from these issues? Are there some common themes and lessons to be drawn from this discussion of disparate contemporary dilemmas in health law? This chapter argues that there *are* things to be learned. The different stories, issues and dilemmas that populate the landscape of contemporary health law and ethics make up the individual pieces that together form the rich kaleidoscope that is contemporary society.

Science Meets Law

After a lengthy period during which the logic of the market economy demanded a retreat from state regulation, the state is now in the process of being reborn. As John Ralston Saul has commented, 'Everywhere you look there are quiet, discreet signs of reregulation' (2005: 200). Medical science and technology are increasingly the focus of this renewed state regulation. This is hardly surprising given the complexities of negotiating between the positive and negative possibilities offered by medical science.

A large part of the appeal of science, and correspondingly of the new technologies of genetics, reproductive technologies and others, lies in the apparent objective and neutral nature of scientific reasoning. The notion that science is simply about discovery, the uncovering of new areas, or the provision of new, objective explanations for the world around us remains strong. Yet science does not exist in a social vacuum. Both the nature of the scientific enterprise and the use of scientific results are deeply embedded in and defined by cultural and historical specificities (Harding 1986). As Dreyfuss and Nelkin point out:

> In fact, the history of science and numerous contemporary studies suggest that the choice of research topics, the nature of scientific theories, and the representation of research results are socially constructed, shaped by cultural forces, and defined to reflect the priorities and assumptions of particular societies at particular times. Furthermore, scientific information is interpreted and applied in a political context and is filtered through social lenses. [1992: 339]

While science appears as value neutral, in fact it cannot divorce itself from its social setting. As Dreyfuss and Nelkin point out, the fact that science is not value neutral does not mean that scientific arguments should be rejected. They argue that it does however mean that 'science-based claims must be parsed with care before they are incorporated into the fabric of the law' (ibid.: 341). Similar caution must be exercised with respect to science's appeal based on its ability to provide predictability or certainty (ibid.: 342–4).

While it is important to be cautious about an uncritical acceptance of scientific explanations for human behaviour, it is equally important to be cautious about an uncritical acceptance of legal reasoning. Like science, law espouses the values of neutrality and objectivity. Like science, the reality of this objectivity has been questioned (see, for example, Frug 1992; Graycar and Morgan 1990; Sheldon and Thomson 1998; Williams 1991). Feminist and critical scholars have been at pains to reveal the assumptions inherent in the processes of legal reasoning and to posit alternative interpretations and meanings. With the potential joining of scientific and legal reasoning, it is critically important to remember that neither discipline can exist outside its social setting.

There is undoubtedly a certain appeal in simple categories and biological explanations. They are, after all, so much easier than the shifting sands of cultural interpretation. Yet while the basic building blocks of our body (tissue, blood, skin and organs) have changed little over time, the significance and meanings ascribed to that body have not proved immutable. Just as notions of gender, race, beauty, or other attributes of identity are culturally and historically specific, so too is our understanding of the basic biology of the human body. In seeking to formulate responses to medical science, it is important not to fall back on essentialist explanations of identity.

There is no doubt that we will need suitable regulatory frameworks to help us in negotiating the path to the future. This argument in favour of regulation is not simply the lawyer's call for more laws, as tempting as this may be. Rather, it is a recognition of the diversity and complexity of contemporary society and of the need for us to find common ground for the way forward. Laws are never just a set of rules devoid of social meaning. In making our regulatory choices, we are making choices over the kind of society we want to have and the values that we hold dear. There are a range of regulatory possibilities that we might choose from, ranging from no regulation through to highly regulated systems. Making choices between these options will not be easy and, given the complexity of the issues involved and the difficulties of achieving community consensus, it may seem easier to avoid regulatory questions and to simply wait for the technology to develop further and for a community consensus to emerge. We need to appreciate, however, that on the technological frontier that failing to regulate is to make a choice. As Michael Kirby has pointed out, 'in these fields, not to do anything is, effectively, to make a decision. It is to accept that science and technology may take our societies where they will' (2003: 16). Fukuyama makes a similar point when he says that 'to not act under conditions of rapid technological change is in effect to make a decision legitimizing that change' (2002: 211). As Roger Brownsword has observed, even 'non-regulation must give some normative signal (whether of prohibition or permission)' (2004a: 15).

The pace of scientific change presents particular challenges for the crafting of new laws for the technological frontier. As we seek to craft these laws, we need to ensure that our legal structures are adequate for the regulatory task at hand. We will need to have flexible laws that can respond rapidly to change, we will need to involve the public so that the community has a sense of ownership in any new laws, we will need to hold true to the value of compromise in decision-making and will need to negotiate the complex terrain of autonomy and choice in contemporary society. Finally, we will need to understand the place of national and state/provincial laws in a globalized economy.

Incremental and Flexible Change

Our society has already benefited enormously from advances in science and medicine. We want to be able to continue to benefit from further advances in the future. Yet we cannot simply rush headlong into the future without thought of where we are going or how we are going to get there. Rapid technological change can create community unease, particularly when the change in question appears to tinker with the very building-blocks of life. We will need to regulate incrementally, making choices about the practices that are acceptable and can be permitted, and those practices that have not yet achieved general acceptance and which should either be subject to greater regulation or be prohibited. Fukuyama has argued that regulation is 'the act of drawing a series of red lines that separate legal from proscribed activities' (2002: 207). While the act of drawing lines is important, we need not draw those lines in permanent marker. Where we draw those lines can change over time and indeed it will be important to develop regulatory structures that can respond to changing community attitudes.

Flexibility will be just as important if we are to be able to be responsive to changes in science and technology. Law generally does have a responsive role with new laws being developed and implemented in response to technological change. It is difficult to craft anticipatory laws for times of rapid scientific and technological change and so the law generally lags behind, with the 'law, marching with medicine but in the rear and limping a little'.[1] To take account of this lag, it is all the more important to ensure that regulatory structures are flexible and responsive to technological change. The inclusion of fixed definitions within legislation can lead to difficulties and regulatory gaps if the science moves on and the definition no longer covers the full range of scientific possibilities. We may choose to regulate using regulatory forms such as guidelines that are easier to change than legislation. We may choose to legislate but require that the legislation is reviewed regularly. Or we may leave the fine detail of regulatory decision-making to a statutory authority with the task of interpreting and implementing broad regulatory goals backed by legislation. Whichever regulatory option we choose, flexibility and the ability to respond rapidly to new science must be key features of any regulatory system for new science. Without that flexibility, any laws we write will soon be outdated and irrelevant. Yet the goal of flexibility

1 *Mount Isa Mines v. Pusey* (1970) 125 CLR 383.

also presents its own difficulties. As Brownsword has pointed out, 'features geared for connection and flexibility tend to militate against predictability and consistency' (2004a: 31). Furthermore, regular reviews of legislation to ensure that connection is maintained, also lead to 'a period of regulatory uncertainty which, arguably, serves to chill investment and research initiatives' (ibid.). A key issue here is the balancing of needs and interests and the need to ensure that the law keeps pace with broader social changes.

While regulatory choices in liberal democratic societies are often structured on social and political compromise, increasingly the battlelines are drawn in ways that make compromise difficult (for discussion, see Brownsword 2004b). The non-negotiability of ethical viewpoints over a range of key issues including the moral status of the embryo, the ethics of the use of cloning technologies, the right to life and the right to die all make for complex and seemingly impossible regulatory choices. Despite these difficulties, compromise remains an important value in our society. It involves making decisions in ways that are respectful not only of the views we hold ourselves, but also of the views held by others. At times, we will be able to reach agreement on core issues. At other times however, agreement may be impossible. In such circumstances, our regulatory solutions may reflect compromise positions that seek to balance not only the differing viewpoints in our community but also the broader community interests at stake. The striking of compromise may seem idealistic given that much of the debate in contemporary society around key issues appears to be polarized, yet in a pluralistic society such as ours, it is important for us to affirm and reaffirm our commitment to respect for differing viewpoints. Indeed, a relational understanding of health law requires that respect for differing viewpoints is a key element in both law reform and regulatory outcomes.

Public Involvement and Ownership

It is likely that in many instances the law and regulation will follow rather than precede scientific developments. While the nature of scientific developments may pose ethical issues for us, the responses that we choose to make to those developments involve political, social and policy choices (Fukuyama 2002: 186). For this reason, we will need to be sure that we have the mechanisms in place for engaging the public with regulatory choices.

At the heart of the difficulty of uniting scientific and social discourses about risk and new technologies is the fact that 'they apply essentially different *epistemologies* to such questions [of risk]' (Hendry 2002: 181). These tensions and uncertainties meet in the regulatory arena where the public increasingly demands involvement in the determination of laws and policies around medical science. In the face of competing and conflicting demands around science, economic interests and public interests, '[t]he task of regulation is to find a way of reconciling those demands. Public trust is the key measure of its political success or failure' (Jones and Salter 2003: 22).

The uncertainty of science on the technological frontier presents major dilemmas for policy-makers and regulators. A number of different discourses weave together in unruly ways that, although providing a rich discursive tapestry, leave us no closer to knowing whether we have made the right regulatory choices. If we are to move past this impasse, there needs to be a new and revitalized dialogue between science and the public: 'Today's public expects not merely to know what is going on, but to be consulted; science is beginning to see the wisdom of this, and...engage in dialogue aimed at mutual understanding' (House of Lords Select Committee on Science and Technology 2000: para. 5.1). We need to recast the relationship between science and society into a more interactive one, opening up possibilities for engagement (ibid.; Jones and Salter 2003). James Surowiecki (2004) has argued that crowds can make better choices and decisions than a small, elite few. This argument suggests that we should seek to engage the public as widely as possible and that we should endeavour to foster opportunities for experts to collaborate and interact locally, nationally and globally. In short, we need to find increased opportunities for science and society to interact over the meaning of scientific possibilities and their significance in contemporary law and society.

Law reform commissions and regulatory agencies have long played an important role both in educating the public about complex issues and in engaging the public in regulatory choices through the publication of public consultation documents, the holding of public fora for discussion, and the call for public submissions. These opportunities for public involvement in key regulatory decisions and for a sense of public ownership in the result represent an important element of ensuring the legitimacy of our regulatory frameworks.

Globalization and Regulatory Reach

The laws we craft to deal with new challenges will also be shaped by the realities of globalization. At the state level and at the national level, the development of laws is influenced by broader global developments. Scientific advances in one country alter the scope of the possible around the globe. The type of laws we formulate when we engage in the processes of law reform are also increasingly influenced by developments at the international level. While each country may craft its own laws, we are also increasingly learning from each other and it is commonplace for law reform to involve a comparative exercise analysing the laws of other countries in the area under discussion and their effectiveness.

The laws of individual countries are generally only effective within each country's jurisdictional boundaries. This means that even if one country's laws comprehensively regulate an area, such as stem cell research or genetic technologies, the effectiveness of those laws ends at the borders. Many countries are likely to have no legislation regulating these technologies. For developed countries, this may be because of the difficulties in achieving a sufficient degree of community agreement on the core issues or for other political reasons. In developing countries, it is unlikely that high-tech issues will be a regulatory priority. Already, individual countries have taken quite different regulatory approaches to the issues surrounding cloning technologies and stem cell research. Although international consensus and regulatory harmonization around these issues is likely to be difficult to achieve, it is none the less important that we continue to engage in dialogue at the global level for it is only by doing so that we will be able to develop an understanding of our points of agreement and disagreement. And it is only from this understanding that international consensus around the ethical challenges can emerge.

It is important for us to recognize that globalization itself is changing. The logic of economic rationalism that fuelled the collapsing of global spaces is no longer as self-evident. While globalization promised a world without borders, the growth of nationalism reveals not only that borders continue to have significance, but that they are also increasingly important (Saul 2005: 203). Indeed, as Saul points out, 'By the end of the twentieth century, nationalism and the nation-states were stronger than they had been when Globalization began' (ibid.: 243). Yet even while nationalism flourishes as new countries emerge and seek recognition, the rapid movement of people between countries may take us to a new, more complex, layered and flexible understanding of belonging (ibid.: 279). What this means for global regulation in the health law context remains to be seen. However, in thinking about regulation, we need to look beyond our immediate horizons and appreciate the ways that people interact both within and across borders and understand that people, countries and regions are connected in multiple ways.

There is no doubt that the complexities of contemporary health and law demand a careful crafting of any policy and regulatory responses. There is no one issue or perspective that provides the path to the future. Rather, we must seek new connections and new patterns. These connections may at first seem unlikely but, as anyone who has ever looked though a kaleidoscope knows, these connections can provide new patterns and new possibilities.

Bibliography

Cases

Attorney-General v. X [1992] ILRM 401
Chatterton v. Gerson [1981] 1 QB 432
Collins v. Wilcock [1984] 1 All ER 1172
Davis v. Davis 842 SW 2d 588 (Tenn 1992)
Dobson v. North Tyneside Health Authority [1997] 1 WLR 596
Dobson (Litigation Guardian of) v. Dobson (1999) 174 DLR (4th) 1
Doodeward v. Spence (1908) 6 CLR 406
Ex Parte Blood [1997] 2 All ER 687 (CA)
Gillick v. West Norfolk and Wisbech Area Health Authority [1986] AC 112
Jefferson v. Griffin Spalding County Hospital Authority (1981) Ga 274 SE 2d 457
McBain v. State of Victoria & Ors (2000) 99 FCR 116
Moore v. Regents of the University of California 793 P 2d 479 (1990)
Mount Isa Mines Ltd v. Pusey (1970) 125 CLR 383
Pearce v. South Australian Health Commission (1996) 66 SASR 486
R v. Kelly [1998] 3 All ER 741
R (on the application of Quintavalle) v. Secretary of State for Health [2001] EWHC Admin 918
R (on the application of Quintavalle) v. Secretary of State for Health [2002] EWCA Civ. 29
Rogers v. Whitaker [1992] 175 CLR 479
Secretary, Department of Health and Community Services v. JWB and SMB (Marion's Case) [1991–92] 175 CLR 218
St George's Healthcare NHS Trust v. S; R v. Collins and Others, ex parte S [1998] 3 All ER 673 (CA)
Winnipeg Child and Family Services (Northwest Area) v. G(D.F.) (1997) 152 DLR (4th) 193

Legislation

Australia

(*Australia – Commonwealth*)

Commonwealth of Australia Constitution Act 1900 (Cth)
Family Law Act 1975 (Cth)
Gene Technology Act 2000 (Cth)
Prohibition of Human Cloning Act 2002 (Cth)

Prohibition of Human Cloning for Reproduction Act 2002 (Cth)
Prohibition of Human Cloning for Reproduction and the Regulation of Human Embryo Research Amendment Act 2006 (Cth)
Research Involving Human Embryos Act 2002 (Cth)
Sex Discrimination Act 1984 (Cth)

(*Australian Capital Territory*)

Human Cloning and Embryo Research Act 2004 (ACT)
Parentage Act 2004 (ACT)
Transplantation and Anatomy Act 1978 (ACT)

(*New South Wales*)

Assisted Reproductive Technology Act 2007 (NSW)
Human Cloning for Reproduction and Other Prohibited Practices Act 2003 (NSW)
Human Tissue Act 1983 (NSW)
Research Involving Human Embryos (New South Wales) Act 2003 (NSW)
Status of Children Act 1996 (NSW)

(*Northern Territory*)

Human Tissue Transplant Act 1979 (NT)
Status of Children Act 1978 (NT)

(*Queensland*)

Research Involving Human Embryos and Prohibition of Human Cloning for Reproduction Act 2003 (Qld)
Status of Children Act 1978 (Qld)
Transplantation and Anatomy Act 1979 (Qld)

(*South Australia*)

Family Relationships Act 1975 (SA)
Prohibition of Human Cloning Act 2003 (SA)
Reproductive Technology (Clinical Practices) Act 1988 (SA)
Reproductive Technology (Code of Ethical Clinical Practice) Regulations 1995 (SA)
Research Involving Human Embryos Act 2003 (SA)
Transplantation and Anatomy Act 1983 (SA)

(*Tasmania*)

Human Cloning and Other Prohibited Practices Act 2003 (Tas)
Human Embryonic Research Regulation Act 2003 (Tas)
Human Tissue Act 1985 (Tas)
Status of Children Act 1974 (Tas)

(Victoria)

Human Tissue Act 1982 (Vic)
Infertility (Medical Procedures) Act 1984 (Vic)
Infertility Treatment Act 1995 (Vic)
Status of Children Act 1974 (Vic)

(Western Australia)

Artificial Conception Act 1985 (WA)
Births, Deaths and Marriages Registration Act 1998 (WA)
Human Reproductive Technology Act 1991 (WA)
Human Tissue and Transplantation Act 1982 (WA)

Britain

Human Fertilisation and Embryology Act 1990 (UK)
Human Fertilisation and Embryology Bill [HL]
Human Reproductive Cloning Act 2004 (UK)

Canada

Assisted Human Reproduction Act (2004) (Canada)

Europe

Council of Europe, Convention for the Protection of Human Rights and Dignity of the Human Being with Regard to the Application of Biology and Medicine (Convention of Human Rights and Biomedicine) (1997)
Council of Europe, Additional Protocol to the Convention for the Protection of Human Rights and Dignity of the Human Being with Regard to the Application of Biology and Medicine, on the Prohibition of Cloning Human Beings (1998)

International

United Nations, Convention on the Rights of the Child (1989)
United Nations General Assembly, United Nations Declaration on Human Cloning (59/280) (2005)
UNESCO, Universal Declaration on Bioethics and Human Rights (2005)
UNESCO, Universal Declaration on the Human Genome and Human Rights (1997)
World Health Organisation, International Health Regulations (2005)

New Zealand

Human Assisted Reproductive Technology Act 2004 (NZ)

References

Achilles, R. (1992), *Donor Insemination: An Overview* (London, Ontario, Canada: Royal Commission on New Reproductive Technologies).

Ahmad, O. (2005), 'Managing Medical Migration from Poor Countries', *British Medical Journal* 331, 43–5.

Albury, R. (1989), 'Inquiring into Ethics: The Australian Senate and Human Embryo Experimentation', *Australian Journal of Social Issues* 24:4, 269–84.

American College of Obstetricians and Gynecologists (2007), *Committee Opinion No. 360: Sex Selection.*

Anderson, M.T. (2000), 'Criminal Penalties for Women Engaging in Substance Abuse During Pregnancy', *Women's Rights Law Reporter* 21, 181–8.

Annas, G. (1990), 'Mapping the Human Genome and the Meaning of Monster Mythology', *Emory Law Journal* 39, 629–64.

—— (2002), 'Bioeterrorism, Public Health and Civil Liberties', *New England Journal of Medicine* 346, 1337–42.

Annas, G., Andrews, L., and Isasi, R.M. (2002), 'Protecting the Endangered Human: Toward an International Treaty Prohibiting Cloning and Inheritable Alterations', *American Journal of Law and Medicine* 28, 151–78.

Asch, A. (1999), 'Prenatal Diagnosis and Selective Abortion: A Challenge to Practice and Policy', *American Journal of Public Health* 89, 1649–57.

Ashcroft, R. (2005), 'Making Sense of Dignity', *Journal of Medical Ethics* 31, 679–82.

Ashe, M. (1988), 'Law-Language of Maternity: Discourse Holding Nature in Contempt', *New England Law Review* 22, 521–59.

Association of Reproductive Health Professionals, *Human Cloning and Genetic Modification: The Basic Science You Need to Know* <http://www.arhp.org/files/cloning.pdf>, accessed 8 March 2007.

Australian Government (2005), *Legislation Review: Prohibition of Human Cloning Act 2002 and the Research Involving Human Embryos Act 2002 Reports* (Canberra: Commonwealth of Australia).

Australian Law Reform Commission (2003), *Essentially Yours: The Protection of Human Genetic Information in Australia* (Report No. 96).

—— (2004), *Genes and Ingenuity: Gene Patenting and Human Health* (Report No. 99).

Baker, R. (1998a), 'A Theory of International Bioethics: Multiculturalism, Postmodernism and the Bankruptcy of Fundamentalism', *Kennedy Institute of Ethics Journal* 8:3, 201–31.

—— (1998b), 'Negotiating International Bioethics: A Response to Tom Beauchamp and Ruth Macklin', *Kennedy Institute of Ethics Journal* 8:4, 423–53.

Bannister, J. (2004), 'Shortage of Girls in China Today', *Journal of Population Research* 21:1, 19–45.

Barritt, J.A., Brenner C.A., Malter, H.E. and Cohen, J. (2001), 'Mitochondria in Human Offspring Derived From Ooplasmic Transplantation', *Human Reproduction* 16:3, 513–16.

Barry, J. (2004), *The Great Influenza: The Epic Story of the Deadliest Plague in History* (New York: Penguin Books).

Baxi, U. (1998), 'Voices of Suffering and the Future of Human Rights', *Transnational Law and Contemporary Problems* 8:2, 125–69.

Bayer, R. and Fairchild, A. (2004), 'The Genesis of Public Health Ethics', *Bioethics* 18:6, 473–92.

Beauchamp, T. and Childress, J. (1989), *Principles of Biomedical Ethics*, 3rd edn (New York: Oxford University Press).

Beauchamp, T.L. (1998), 'The Mettle of Moral Fundamentalism: A Reply to Robert Baker', *Kennedy Institute of Ethics Journal* 8:4, 389–401.

Beck, U. (1992), *Risk Society: Towards a New Modernity* (translated by Mark Ritter) (London: Sage).

—— (2000), *What is Globalization?* (translated by Patrick Camiller) (Cambridge: Polity Press).

Beem, P. (2004), 'Where Does a Man Stand on Issues of Assisted Reproduction, Surrogacy, Artificial Insemination Within Lesbian Relationships and Posthumous Conception?' *Australian Journal of Family Law* 18:1, 1–28.

Bell, D. (1999), 'Human Cloning and International Human Rights Law', *Sydney Law Review* 21, 202–30.

Bender, L. (1992), 'A Feminist Analysis of Physician-Assisted Dying and Voluntary Active Euthanasia', *Tennessee Law Review* 59, 519–46.

Benatar, S., Daar, A.S., and Singer, P.A. (2003), 'Global Health Ethics: The Rationale for Mutual Caring', *International Affairs* 79:1, 107–38.

Bennett, B. (2005), 'Symbiotic Relationships: Saviour Siblings, Family Rights and Biomedicine', *Australian Journal of Family Law* 19:3, 195–212.

—— (2006), 'Travel in a Small World: SARS, Globalization and Public Health Laws', in B. Bennett and G.F. Tomossy (eds) (2006), *Globalization and Health: Challenges for Health Law and Bioethics* (Dordrecht: Springer), 1–12.

—— and Tomossy, G.F. (eds) (2006), *Globalization and Health: Challenges for Health Law and Bioethics* (Dordrecht: Springer).

Beyleveld, D. and Brownsword, R. (1998), 'Human Dignity, Human Rights and Human Genetics', *Modern Law Review* 61:5, 661–80.

Black, J. (1995), '"Which Arrow?" Rule Type and Regulatory Policy', *Public Law* Spring 1995, 94–117.

Blood, D. (2005), *Flesh and Blood: The Harrowing and Moving Story of a Mother's Fight to Bear Her Late Husband's Children* (Edinburgh: Mainstream Publishing).

Bodmer, W. and McKie, R. (1994), *The Book of Man: The Quest to Discover Our Genetic Heritage* (London: Little Brown).

Booy, R., Brown, L.E., Grohmann, G.S. and MacIntyre, C.R. (2006), 'Pandemic Vaccines: Promises and Pitfalls', *Medical Journal of Australia* 185, S62–5.

Bostrom, N. (2005), 'In Defense of Posthuman Dignity', *Bioethics* 19:3, 202–14.

Botkin, J. (1998), 'Ethical Issues and Practical Problems in Preimplantation Genetic Diagnosis', *Journal of Law, Medicine and Ethics* 26, 17–28.

Boyle, J. (2003), 'The Second Enclosure Movement and the Construction of the Public Domain', *Law and Contemporary Problems* 66, 33–74.

Braude, P., Minger, S.L., and Warwick, R.M. (2005), 'Stem Cell Therapy: Hope or Hype?', *British Medical Journal* 330, 1159–60.

Brazier, M. (1999), 'Regulating the Reproduction Business?', *Medical Law Review* 7:2, 166–93.

Brock, D. (2001), 'Some Questions About the Moral Responsibilities of Drug Companies in Developing Countries', *Developing World Bioethics* 1:1, 33–7.

Brooks, G. (2002), *Year of Wonders: A Novel of the Plague* (London: Fourth Estate).

Brownsword, R. (2003), 'Bioethics Today, Bioethics Tomorrow: Stem Cell Research and the "Dignitarian Alliance"', *Notre Dame Journal of Law, Ethics and Public Policy* 17:1, 15–52.

—— (2004a), 'Regulating Human Genetics: New Dilemmas for a New Millennium', *Medical Law Review* 12:1, 14–39.

—— (2004b), 'Reproductive Opportunities and Regulatory Challenges', *Modern Law Review* 67:2, 304–21.

Brundtland, G. (2003), 'Global Health and International Security', *Global Governance* 9:4, 417–23.

Bubela, T. and Caulfield, T.A. (2004), 'Do the Print Media "Hype" Genetic Research? A Comparison of Newspaper Stories and Peer-reviewed Research Papers', *Canadian Medical Association Journal* 170:9, 1399–1407.

Buchanan, A., Brock, D.W., Daniels, N. and Wikler D. (2000), *From Chance to Choice: Genetics & Justice* (New York: Cambridge University Press).

Byrne, E. and Howells, D. (2003), 'Stem Cell Therapies: A Tale of Caution', *Medical Journal of Australia* 179:3, 164–6.

Cameron, P.A., Rainer, T.H. and Smit, P.D.V. (2003), 'The SARS Epidemic: Lessons for Australia', *Medical Journal of Australia* 178, 478–9.

Campbell, A. and Glass, K. (2001), 'The Legal Status of Clinical and Ethics Policies, Codes and Guidelines in Medical Practice and Research', *McGill Law Journal* 46:2, 473–90.

Campbell, A. and Nycum, G. (2005), 'Harmonizing the International Regulation of Embryonic Stem Cell Research: Possibilities, Promises and Potential Pitfalls', *Medical Law International* 7:2, 113–48.

Cannold, L. (1998), *The Abortion Myth: Feminism, Morality and the Hard Choices Women Make* (St Leonards, Sydney: Allen and Unwin).

Canoles, M.E. (2002), 'Italy's Family Values: Embracing the Evolution of Family to Save the Population', *Penn State International Law Review* 21, 183–204.

Caulfield, T. and Brownsword, R. (2006), 'Human Dignity: A Guide to Policy Making in the Biotechnology Era?', *Nature Reviews Genetics* 7:1, 72–6.

Caulfield, T., Knowles, L. and Meslin, E.M. (2004), 'Law and Policy in the Era of Reproductive Genetics', *Journal of Medical Ethics* 30:4, 414–17.

Chalmers, Damian (2003), '"Food for Thought": Reconciling European Risks and Traditional Ways of Life', *Modern Law Review* 66:4, 532–62.

Chalmers, Donald (1999), 'The Challenges of Human Genetics', in I. Freckelton and K. Petersen (eds), *Controversies in Health Law* (Sydney: Federation Press), 202–39.

—— (2002), 'Professional Self-Regulation and Guidelines in Assisted Reproduction', *Journal of Law and Medicine* 9:4, 414–28.

Charlesworth, H. and Chinkin, C. (2000), *The Boundaries of International Law: A Feminist Analysis* (Manchester: Manchester University Press).

Charo, R. (1992–93), 'And Baby Makes Three – or Four, or Five, or Six: Redefining the Family After the Reprotech Revolution', *Wisconsin Women's Law Journal* 7, 1–23.

Childress, J. and Bernheim, R. (2003), 'Beyond the Liberal and Communitarian Impasse: A Framework and Vision for Public Health', *Florida Law Review* 55:5, 1191–219.

Collignon, P.J. and Carnie, J.A. (2006), 'Infection Control and Pandemic Influenza', *Medical Journal of Australia* 185, S54–7.

Committee to Consider the Social, Ethical and Legal Issues Arising from In Vitro Fertilisation (1984), *Report on the Disposition of Embryos Produced by In Vitro Fertilisation* (Melbourne: Victorian Government Printer).

Connolly, M., Gayer, M., Ryan, M.J., Salama, P., Spiegel, P., and Heymann, D.L. (2004), 'Communicable Diseases in Complex Emergencies: Impacts and Challenges', *Lancet* 364:9449, 1974–83.

Cook, R.J. (1995), 'Human Rights and Reproductive Self-Determination', *American University Law Review* 44, 975–1016.

Cooper, D. (2006), 'The Lockhart Review: Where Now for Australia?', *Journal of Law and Medicine* 14:1, 27–44.

Cooper, D. and Herman, D. (1991), '"Getting the Family Right": Legislating Heterosexuality in Britain, 1986–1991', *Canadian Journal of Family Law* 10, 41–78.

Croucher, R. (2006) 'Disposing of the Dead: Objectivity, Subjectivity and Identity', in I. Freckelton and K. Petersen (eds), *Disputes and Dilemmas in Health Law* (Annandale, NSW: Federation Press), 324–43.

Daniels, K.R. and Thorn, P. (2001), 'Sharing Information with Donor Insemination Offspring: A Child-Conception Versus a Family-Building Approach', *Human Reproduction* 16:9, 1792–6.

Danis, J. (1995), 'Sexism and the "Superfluous Female": Arguments for Regulating Pre-implantation Sex Selection', *Harvard Women's Law Journal* 18, 219–64.

Darvall, L. (1993), *Medicine, Law and Social Change: The Impact of Bioethics, Feminism and Rights Movements on Medical Decision-making* (Aldershot: Dartmouth Publishing).

Davies, T. (2006), 'Non-voluntary Licensing of Antivirals Under Patent: Options the Australian Government Should Consider in Light of a Potential Bird Flu Pandemic', *Journal of Law and Medicine* 13, 479–95.

DeAngelis, C. and Flanagin, A. (2005), 'Tuberculosis – A Global Problem Requiring a Global Solution', *Journal of the American Medical Association* 293, 2793–4.

Department of Health and Ageing (Australia) (2004), *Protecting Australia from Communicable Diseases: Everybody's Business: A Special Report from the Commonwealth Chief Medical Officer* (Canberra: Department of Health and Ageing).

—— (2005), *Australian Management Plan for Pandemic Influenza*, (Canberra: Commonwealth of Australia).

Department of Health (UK) (2006), *Review of the Human Fertilisation and Embryology Act: Proposals for Revised Legislation (Including Establishment of the Regulatory Authority for Tissues and Embryos)* (London: Department of Health, Cmnd 6989).

Department of Health (Western Australia), *Voluntary Register: Information About Donation in Assisted Reproduction* <http://www.voluntaryregister.health.wa.gov.au>, accessed 22 June 2006.

Dewar, J. (1989), 'Fathers in Law? The Case of AID', in R. Lee and D. Morgan (eds), *Birthrights: Law and Ethics at the Beginnings of Life* (London; New York: Routledge), 115–31.

Diamond, J. (1998), *Guns, Germs and Steel: A Short History of Everybody for the Last 13,000 Years* (London: Vintage).

Dickens, B. (2002), 'Can Sex Selection Be Ethically Tolerated?', *Journal of Medical Ethics* 28, 335–6.

Dickenson, D. (2006), 'The Lady Vanishes: What's Missing from the Stem Cell Debate', *Journal of Bioethical Inquiry* 3, 43–54.

Dolgin, J. (2003), 'Embryonic Discourse: Abortion, Stem Cells, and Cloning', *Florida State University Law Review* 31, 101–62.

Donchin, A. (2001), 'Understanding Autonomy Relationally: Toward a Reconfiguration of Bioethical Principles', *Journal of Medicine and Philosophy* 26:4, 365–86.

Dowd, N. (1995), 'Stigmatizing Single Parents,' *Harvard Women's Law Journal* 18, 19–82.

Dowdeswell, E., Daar, A. and Singer, P. (2003), 'Bridging the Genomics Divide', *Global Governance* 9, 1–6.

Dower, T. (2001), 'Redefining Family: Should Lesbians Have Access to Assisted Reproduction?', *Melbourne University Law Review* 25, 466–80.

Dreyfuss, R. and Nelkin, D. (1992), 'The Jurisprudence of Genetics', *Vanderbilt Law Review* 45:2, 313–48.

Erickson, D., Gostin, L.O., Stree, J. and Mills, S.P. (2002), 'The Power to Act: Two Model State Statutes', *Journal of Law, Medicine and Ethics* 30:3, S57–62.

Farmer, P. and Campos, N. (2004), 'New Malaise: Bioethics and Human Rights in the Global Era', *Journal of Law, Medicine and Ethics* 32:2, 243–51.

Faunce, T. (2005), 'Will International Human Rights Subsume Medical Ethics? Intersections in the UNESCO Universal Bioethics Declaration', *Journal of Medical Ethics* 31:3, 173–8.

Fidler, D.P. (2004), *SARS, Governance and the Globalization of Disease* (Basingstoke: Palgrave Macmillan).

—— (2005), 'From International Sanitary Conventions to Global Health Security: The New International Health Regulations', *Chinese Journal of International Law* 4:2, 325–92.

Fidler, D.P. and Gostin, L. (2006), 'The New International Health Regulations: An Historic Development for International Law and Public Health', *Journal of Law, Medicine and Ethics* 34:1, 85–94.

Fineman, M. (1991), 'Images of Mothers in Poverty Discourses', *Duke Law Journal*, 274–95.

—— (1992), 'The Neutered Mother', *University of Miami Law Review* 46, 653–69.

—— (2004), *The Autonomy Myth: A Theory of Dependency* (New York: The New Press).

Finley, L. (1989), 'Breaking Women's Silence in Law: The Dilemma of the Gendered Nature of Legal Reasoning', *Notre Dame Law Review* 64:5, 886–910.

Francis, L.P., Battin, M.P., Jacobson, J.A., Smith, C.B. and Botkin, J. (2005), 'How Infectious Diseases Got Left Out – And What This Omission Might Have Meant For Bioethics', *Bioethics* 19:4, 307–22.

Frenk, J. and Gómez-Dantés, O. (2002), 'Globalisation and the Challenges to Health Systems', *British Medical Journal* 325, 95–7.

Friedman, T. (2005), *The World is Flat: A Brief History of the Twenty-First Century* (New York: Farrar, Straus and Giroux).

Frug, M. (1992), *Postmodern Legal Feminism* (New York: Routledge).

Fukuyama, F. (2002), *Our Posthuman Future: Consequences of the Biotechnology Revolution* (New York: Picador).

Gamble, H. (1990), 'Fathers and the New Reproductive Technologies: Recognition of the Donor as Parent', *Australian Journal of Family Law* 4:2, 131–44.

Gaze, B. (1992), 'Controlling Medical Science: Reproductive Technology, Infertility and the Position of Women', *Law in Context* 10, 29–55.

Gensini, G.F., Yacoub, M.H. and Conti, A.A. (2004), 'The Concept of Quarantine in History: From Plague to SARS', *Journal of Infection* 49:4, 257–61.

Giddens, A. (1999), 'Risk and Responsibility', *Modern Law Review* 62:1, 1–10.

Gilligan, C. (1982), *In a Different Voice: Psychological Theory and Women's Development* (Cambridge, MA: Harvard University Press).

Glaister, D. (2007), '"Holy Moly" – Sperm Donor Comes Faces to Face With His Children 20 Years Later', the *Guardian*, 16 February 2007.

Golombok, S. and Rust, J. (1986), 'The Warnock Report and Single Women: What About the Children?', *Journal of Medical Ethics* 12, 182–6.

Goodwin, M. (2006), *Black Markets: The Supply and Demand of Body Parts* (New York: Cambridge University Press).

Gostin, L. (2000), *Public Health Law: Power, Duty, Restraint* (Berkeley: University of California Press).

—— (2002), 'Public Health Law: A Renaissance', *Journal of Law, Medicine and Ethics* 30, 136–40.

—— (2004), 'Pandemic Influenza: Public Health Preparedness for the Next Global Health Emergency', *Journal of Law, Medicine and Ethics* 32, 565–72.

—— (2006), 'Medical Countermeasures for Pandemic Influenza: Ethics and the Law', *Journal of the American Medical Association* 295, 554–6.

—— (2007), 'Meeting the Survival Needs of the World's Least Healthy People: A Proposed Model for Global Health Governance', *JAMA* 298:2, 225–8.

—— Bayer, R. and Fairchild, A.L. (2003), 'Ethical and Legal Challenges Posed by Severe Acute Respiratory Syndrome: Implications for the Control of Severe Infectious Disease Threats', *Journal of the American Medical Association* 290, 3229–37.

Gostin, L., Sapsin, J.W., Teret, S.P., Burris S., Mair, J.S., Hodge, J.G. and Vernick, J.S. (2002), 'The Model State Emergency Health Powers Act: Planning for and Response to Bioterrorism and Naturally Occurring Infectious Diseases', *Journal of the American Medical Association* 288, 622–8.

Gottlieb, C., Lalos, O. and Lindblad, F. (2000), 'Disclosure of Donor Insemination to the Child: The Impact of Swedish Legislation on Couples' Attitudes', *Human Reproduction* 15:9, 2052–6.

Goyal, M., Mehta, R.L., Schneiderman, L.J. and Sehgal, A.R. (2002), 'Economic and Health Consequences of Selling a Kidney in India', *Journal of the American Medical Association* 288:13, 1589–93.

Graycar, R. and Morgan, J. (1992), *The Hidden Gender of Law* (Annandale, NSW: Federation Press).

Green, R. (1997), 'Parental Autonomy and the Obligation Not to Harm One's Child Genetically', *Journal of Law, Medicine and Ethics* 25:1, 5–15.

Greenfield, S. (2003), *Tomorrow's People: How 21st Century Technology is Changing the Way We Think and Feel* (London: Penguin Books).

Griggs, L. (1994), 'The Ownership of Excised Body Parts: Does an Individual Have the Right to Sell?' *Journal of Law and Medicine* 1, 223–8.

Gudorf, C. (1996), 'Gender and Culture in the Globalization of Bioethics', *St Louis University Public Law Review* 15, 331–51.

Gunning, J. and Szoke, H. (eds) (2003), *The Regulation of Assisted Reproductive Technology* (Aldershot: Ashgate).

Haimes, E. (1988), '"Secrecy": What Can Artificial Reproduction Learn From Adoption?', *International Journal of Law and the Family* 2, 46–61.

—— (1990), 'Recreating the Family? Policy Considerations Relating to the "New" Reproductive Technologies', in M. McNeil, I. Varcoe and S. Yearley (eds), *The New Reproductive Technologies* (London: Macmillan), 154–72.

—— (2002), 'When Transgressions Become Transparent: Limiting Family Forms in Assisted Conception', *Journal of Law and Medicine* 9, 438–48.

Halliday, S. (2004), 'A Comparative Approach to the Regulation of Human Embryonic Stem Cell Research in Europe', *Medical Law Review* 12, 40–69.

Hamilton, C. and Denniss, R. (2005), *Affluenza: When Too Much is Never Enough* (Crows Nest, NSW: Allen & Unwin).

Harding, S. (1996), *The Science Question in Feminism* (Ithaca, NY: Cornell University Press).

Harrington, J. (2006), 'Globalization and English Medical Law', in B. Bennett and G.F. Tomossy (eds), *Globalization and Health: Challenges for Health Law and Bioethics* (Dordrecht: Springer), 169–85.

Harris, J., Bortolotti, L. and Irving, L. (2005), 'An Ethical Framework for Stem Cell Research in the European Union' *Health Care Analysis* 13:3, 157–62.

Hartouni, V. (1997), *Cultural Conceptions: On Reproductive Technologies and the Remaking of Life* (Minneapolis: University of Minnesota Press).

Häyry, M. (2004), 'There is a Difference Between Selecting a Deaf Embryo and Deafening a Hearing Child', *Journal of Medical Ethics* 30, 510–12.

Held, D., McGrew, A., Goldblatt, D. and Perraton, J. (1999), *Global Transformations: Politics, Economics and Culture* (Cambridge: Polity Press).

Heller, M. and Eisenberg, R. (1998), 'Can Patents Deter Innovation? The Anticommons in Biomedical Research', *Science* 280, 698–701.

Hendry, C. (2002), 'Science, Industry and the Laity: Towards a Knowledgeable Society for Biotechnology', *New Genetics and Society* 21:2, 177–98.

Hervey, T. (1998), 'Buy Baby: The European Union and Regulation of Human Reproduction', *Oxford Journal of Legal Studies* 18, 207–33.

—— and McHale, J. (2004), *Health Law and the European Union* (Cambridge: Cambridge University Press).

Hinxton Group, *Consensus Statement* (24 February 2006) <http://www.hopkinsmedicine.org/bioethics/finalsc.doc>, accessed 3 January 2008.

House of Commons Science and Technology Committee (2005), *Human Reproductive Technologies and the Law* (Fifth Report of Session 2004–05) (London: The Stationery Office Ltd).

House of Lords Select Committee on Science and Technology (2000), *Science and Technology – Third Report* (Third Report of Session 1999–2000) (UK Parliament).

House of Representatives Standing Committee on Legal and Constitutional Affairs (2001), *Human Cloning: Scientific, Ethical and Regulatory Aspects of Human Cloning and Stem Cell Research* (Canberra: Commonwealth of Australia).

Human Fertilisation and Embryology Authority (2005), *Tomorrow's Children: Report of the Policy Review of Welfare of the Child Assessments in Licensed Assisted Conception Clinics* (London: Human Fertilisation and Embryology Authority).

—— (2006), *The HFEA Guide to Infertility 2006/07* (London: Human Fertilisation and Embryology Authority).

Human Fertilisation and Embryology Authority and Human Genetics Advisory Commission (2001), *Outcome of the Public Consultation on Preimplantation Genetic Diagnosis* (London: Human Fertilisation and Embryology Authority).

Human Genetics Advisory Commission and Human Fertilisation and Embryology Authority (1998), *Cloning Issues in Reproduction, Science and Medicine* (London: Human Genetics Advisory Commission and Human Fertilisation and Embryology Authority).

Human Genetics Commission (2006), *Making Babies: Reproductive Decisions and Genetic Technologies* (London: Human Genetics Commission).

Hurwitz, I. (2000), 'Collaborative Reproduction: Finding the Child in the Maze of Legal Motherhood', *Connecticut Law Review* 33:1, 127–80.

Hyde, A. (1997), *Bodies of Law* (Princeton, NJ: Princeton University Press).

Infertility Treatment Authority (2006), *Donor Conception: Parents Disclosing Donor Conception to Their Children: What Does the Literature Tell Us?* (Melbourne: Infertility Treatment Authority).

—— (2007), 'Central Registers', <http://www.ita.org.au/www/257/1001127/displayarticle/1001410.html>, accessed 5 March 2007.

International Monetary Fund (2006), *The Global Economic and Financial Impact of an Avian Flu Pandemic and the Role of the IMF* <http://www.imf.org/external/pubs/ft/afp/2006/eng/022806.pdf>, accessed 3 January 2008.

Isasi, R. and Nguyen, T. (2005), 'The Global Governance of Infectious Diseases: The World Health Organization and the International Health Regulations', *Alberta Law Review* 43, 497–510.

Itzwerth, R.L., MacIntyre, C.R., Shah, S. and Plant, A.J. (2006), 'Pandemic Influenza and Critical Infrastructure Dependencies: Possible Impact on Hospitals', *Medical Journal of Australia* 185, S70–72.

Jackson, E. (2000), 'Abortion, Autonomy and Prenatal Diagnosis', *Social & Legal Studies* 9:4, 467–94.

—— (2002), 'Conception and the Irrelevance of the Welfare Principle', *Modern Law Review* 65:2, 176–203.

Janssens, P.M.W., Simons, A.H.M., van Kooij, R.J., Blokzijl, E. and Dunselman, G.A.J. (2006), 'A New Dutch Law Regulating Provision of Identifying Information of Donors to Offspring: Background, Content and Impact', *Human Reproduction* 21:4, 852–6.

Johnson, J. (2005), 'Stopping Africa's Medical Brain Drain', *British Medical Journal* 331:7507, 2–3.

Jones, M. and Salter, B. (2003), 'The Governance of Human Genetics: Policy Discourse and Constructions of Public Trust', *New Genetics and Society* 22:1, 21–41.

Juss, S. (1997), 'Global Environmental Change: Health and the Challenge for Human Rights', *Indiana Journal of Global Legal Studies* 5:1, 121–78.

Karpin, I. (1992), 'Legislating the Female Body: Reproductive Technology and the Reconstructed Woman', *Columbia Journal of Gender and Law* 3:1, 325–49.

—— (2000), 'The Genetic Connection: Owning Our "Genetic Heritage"', *Journal of Law and Medicine* 7:4, 376–89.

—— (2006), 'The Uncanny Embryos: Legal Limits to the Human and Reproduction Without Women', *Sydney Law Review* 28, 599–623.

Karpin, I. and O'Connell, K. (2002), 'Intimate Strangers: Law, Genetics, Globalisation and the "Human Family"', *Australian Feminist Law Journal* 17, 63–82.

Kasimba, P. and Buckle, S. (1988), 'Embryos and Children: Problems Raised by the Majority Report of the Senate Select Committee on Human Embryo Experimentation', *Australian Journal of Family Law* 2:3, 228–39.

—— (1989), 'Guardianship and the IVF Human Embryo', *Melbourne University Law Review* 17:1, 139–52.

Keller, E. (1992), 'Nature, Nurture, and the Human Genome Project', in D. Kevles and L. Hood (eds), *The Code of Codes: Scientific and Social Issues in the Human Genome Project* (Cambridge, MA: Harvard University Press), 281–99.

Kelly, M. (2004), *A History of the Black Death in Ireland* (Stroud: Tempus Publishing Ltd).

Kennedy, S.E., Shen, Y., Charlesworth, J.A., Mackie, J.D., Mahony, J.D., Kelly, J.J.P. and Pussell, B.A. (2005), 'Outcome of Overseas Commercial Kidney Transplantation: An Australian Perspective', *Medical Journal of Australia* 182, 224–7.

Kindhauser, M. (ed.) (2003), *Global Defense Against the Infectious Disease Threat* (Geneva: World Health Organisation).

Kirby, M. (2003), 'Genomics and Democracy: A Global Challenge', *Western Australian Law Review* 31:1, 1–18.

Knoppers, B. and LeBris, S. (1991), 'Recent Advances in Medically Assisted Conception: Legal, Ethical and Social Issues', *American Journal of Law and Medicine* 17:4, 329–61.

Knowles, L. (1999), 'Property, Progeny and Patents', *Hastings Center Report* 29:2, 38–40.

Kolata, G. (1997), *Clone: The Road to Dolly and the Path Ahead* (London: Penguin Books).

Kreimer, S. (1992), 'The Law of Choice and Choice of Law: Abortion, The Right to Travel and Extraterritorial Regulation in American Federalism', *New York University Law Review* 67, 451–519.

Kritchevsky, B. (1981), 'The Unmarried Woman's Right to Artificial Insemination: A Call For an Expanded Definition of Family', *Harvard Women's Law Journal* 4, 1–42.

Kurzweil, R. (2005), *The Singularity is Near: When Humans Transcend Biology* (New York: Viking).

Lacey, N. (1998), *Unspeakable Subjects: Feminist Essays in Legal and Social Theory* (Oxford: Hart Publishing).

Laing, J. and Oderberg, D. (2005), 'Artificial Reproduction, the "Welfare Principle" and the Common Good', *Medical Law Review* 13, 328–56.

Laurie, G. (2002), *Genetic Privacy: A Challenge to Medico-Legal Norms* (Cambridge: Cambridge University Press).

Law Commission (New Zealand) (2005), *New Issues in Legal Parenthood* (Report No. 88) (Wellington, New Zealand).

Lee, M.L. (2004), 'The Inadequacies of Absolute Prohibition of Reproductive Cloning', *Journal of Law and Medicine* 11, 351–72.

Lee, N., Hui, D., Wu, A., Chan, P., Cameron, P., Joynt, G.M., Ahuja, A., Yung, M.Y., Leung. C.B., To, K.F., Lui, S.F., Szeto, C.C., Chung, S. and Sung, J.J. (2003), 'A Major Outbreak of Severe Acute Respiratory Syndrome in Hong Kong', *New England Journal of Medicine* 348, 1986–94.

Lee, R.G. and Morgan, D. (2001a), 'Regulating Risk Society: Stigmata Cases, Scientific Citizenship and Biomedical Diplomacy', *Sydney Law Review* 23:3, 297–318.

—— (2001b), *Human Fertilisation and Embryology: Regulating the Reproduction Revolution* (London: Blackstone Press).

Lockhart Review – See Australian Government (2005).

Lycett, E., Daniels, K., Curson, R., Chir, B. and Golombok, S. (2004), 'Offspring Created as a Result of Donor Insemination: A Study of Family Relationships, Child Adjustment, and Disclosure', *Fertility and Sterility* 82:1, 172–9.

Mackenbach, J.P. (2007), 'Sanitation: Pragmatism Works', *British Medical Journal* 334, S17.

Mackenzie, C. (1992), 'Abortion and Embodiment', *Australian Journal of Philosophy* 70:2, 136–55.

—— and Stoljar, N. (2000), *Relational Autonomy: Feminist Perspectives on Autonomy, Agency and the Social Self* (New York, Oxford: Oxford University Press).

Macklin, R. (1998a), 'Ethical Relativism in a Multicultural Society', *Kennedy Institute of Ethics Journal* 8:1, 1–22.

—— (1998b), 'A Defense of Fundamental Principles and Human Rights: A Reply to Robert Baker', *Kennedy Institute of Ethics Journal* 8:4, 403–22.

—— (1999), *Against Relativism: Cultural Diversity and the Search for Ethical Universals in Medicine* (New York: Oxford University Press).

Magnusson, R. (1998), 'Proprietary Rights in Human Tissue', in N. Palmer and E. McKendrick (eds), *Interests in Goods* (London: Lloyd's of London Press), 25–62.

Marriott, E. (2002), *The Plague Race: A Tale of Fear, Science and Heroism* (London: Picador).

Marshall, P. and Koening, B. (2004), 'Accounting for Culture in a Globalized Bioethics', *Journal of Law, Medicine and Ethics* 32:2, 252–66.

Martineau, T., Decker, K. and Bundred, P. (2004), '"Brain Drain" of Health Professionals: From Rhetoric to Responsible Action', *Health Policy* 70:1, 1–10.

Mathew, T., Faull, R. and Snelling, P. (2005), 'The Shortage of Kidneys for Transplantation in Australia', *Medical Journal of Australia* 182, 204–05.

McDougall, R. (2005), 'Acting Parentally: An Argument Against Sex Selection', *Journal of Medical Ethics* 31, 601–605.

McGee, G., Brakman, S.V. and Gurmankin, A.D. (2001), 'Gamete Donation and Anonymity: Disclosure to Children Conceived with Donor Gametes Should Not be Optional', *Human Reproduction* 16, 2033–6.

McKibbin, W. and Sidorenko, A. (2006), *Global Macroceconomic Consequences of Pandemic Influenza* (Sydney: Lowy Institute for International Policy).

McLean, S.A.M. (1998), 'Interventions in the Human Genome', *Modern Law Review* 61:5, 681–96.

McNair, R. (2004), *Outcomes for Children Born of A.R.T. in a Diverse Range of Families* (Melbourne: Victorian Law Reform Commission).

McSherry, B. and Naylor, B. (2004), *Australian Criminal Laws: Critical Perspectives* (Melbourne: Oxford University Press).

McWhinnie, A. (2001), 'Gamete Donation and Anonymity: Should Offspring From Donated Gametes Continue to be Denied Knowledge of Their Origins and Antecedents?', *Human Reproduction* 16:5, 807–17.

Mehlman, M. and Rabe, K. (2002), 'Any DNA to Declare? Regulating Offshore Access to Genetic Enhancement', *American Journal of Law & Medicine* 28, 179–213.

Millbank, J. (2006a), 'Recognition of Lesbian and Gay Families in Australian Law – Part One: Couples', *Federal Law Review* 34, 1–44.

—— (2006b), 'Recognition of Lesbian and Gay Families in Australian Law – Part Two: Children', *Federal Law Review* 34, 205–59.

Millns, S. (2002), 'Reproducing Inequalities: Assisted Conception and the Challenge of Legal Pluralism', *Journal of Social Welfare and Family Law* 24:1, 19–36.

Moazam, F. (2004), 'Feminist Discourse on Sex Screening and Selective Abortion of Female Foetuses', *Bioethics* 18:3, 205–20.

Monahan, G. and Young, L. (2006), *Family Law in Australia* (6th edn) (Sydney: LexisNexis Butterworths).

Morgan, D. (2001), *Issues in Medical Law and Ethics* (London and Sydney: Cavendish).

Motluk, A. (2005), 'Tracing Dad Online', *New Scientist* 188:2524, 6.

Murray, C.J.L., Lopez, A.D., Chin, B., Feehan, D. and Hill, K.H. (2006), 'Estimation of Potential Global Pandemic Influenza Mortality on the Basis of Vital Registry Data from the 1918–20 Pandemic: A Quantitative Analysis', *Lancet* 368, 2211–18.

Mykitiuk, R. (1994), 'Fragmenting the Body', *Australian Feminist Law Journal* 2, 63–98.

Nader, C. (2006), 'Mummy, Daddy and the Donor', *The Age*, 13 May, 3.

Naffine, N. (1997), 'The Body Bag', in N. Naffine and R. Owens (eds), *Sexing the Subject of Law* (North Ryde, NSW: LBC Information Services), 79–93.

—— (1998), 'The Legal Structure of Self-Ownership: Or the Self-Possessed Man and the Woman Possessed', *Journal of Law and Society* 25:2, 193–212.

National Advisory Committee on SARS and Public Health (2003), *Learning from SARS: Renewal of Public Health in Canada* (Ottawa: Health Canada).

National Bioethics Advisory Commission (1997), *Cloning Human Beings: Report and Recommendations of the National Bioethics Advisory Commission* (Rockville, MD: National Bioethics Advisory Commission).

National Bioethics Consultative Committee (1988), *Access to Information: An Analogy Between Adoption and the Use of Gamete Donation* (Canberra: National Bioethics Consultative Committee).

—— (1991), *Access to Reproductive Technology: Final Report for the Australian Health Ministers' Conference* (Canberra: National Bioethics Consultative Committee).

NHMRC (National Health and Medical Research Council) (1996), *Ethical Guidelines on Assisted Reproductive Technology* (Canberra: Australian Government Publishing Service).

—— (2004), *Ethical Guidelines on the Use of Assisted Reproductive Technology in Clinical Practice and Research* (Canberra: National Health and Medical Research Council).

—— (2007a), *Ethical Guidelines on the Use of Assisted Reproductive Technologies in Clinical Practice and Research 2004 (as Revised in 2007 to Take into Account the Changes in Legislation)* (Canberra: Australian Government).

—— (2007b), *National Statement on Ethical Conduct in Human Research* (Canberra: Australian Government).

Nedelsky, J. (1989), 'Reconceiving Autonomy: Sources, Thoughts and Possibilities', *Yale Journal of Law and Feminism* 1, 7–36.

—— (1993), 'Property in Potential Life? A Relational Approach to Choosing Legal Categories', *Canadian Journal of Law and Jurisprudence* 6:2, 343–65.

New South Wales Law Reform Commission (2004), *Issues Paper 24: Minors' Consent to Medical Treatment* (Sydney: NSW Law Reform Commission).

Nichol, D. and Nielsen, J. (2001), 'The Australian Medical Biotechnology Industry and Access to Intellectual Property: Issues for Patent Law Development', *Sydney Law Review* 23:3, 347–74.

Nichol, D., Otlowski, M. and Chalmers, D. (2001), 'Consent, Commercialisation and Benefit-Sharing', *Journal of Law and Medicine* 9:1, 80–94.

Nidadavolu, V. and Bracken, H. (2006), 'Abortion and Sex Determination: Conflicting Messages in Information Materials in a District of Rajasthan, India', *Reproductive Health Matters* 14:27, 160–71.

Note (1985), 'Reproductive Technology and the Procreation Rights of the Unmarried', *Harvard Law Review* 98:3, 669–85.

Nuffield Council on Bioethics (2002), *The Ethics of Research Related to Healthcare in Developing Countries* (London: Nuffield Council on Bioethics).

Nullis-Kapp, C. (2004), 'Organ Trafficking and Transplantation Pose New Challenges', *Bulletin of the World Health Organization* 82:9, 715.

O'Donovan, K. (1989), 'What Shall We Tell The Children? Reflections on Children's Perspectives and the Reproduction Revolution', in R. Lee and D. Morgan (eds), *Birthrights: Law and Ethics at the Beginning of Life* (London and New York: Routledge), 96–114.

Opeskin, B. (1998), 'The Architecture of Public Health Law Reform: Harmonisation of Law in a Federal System', *Melbourne University Law Review* 22:2, 337–69.

Osterholm, M. (2005), 'A Weapon the World Needs', *Nature* 435:7041, 417–18.

Overall, C. (1987), *Ethics and Human Reproduction: A Feminist Analysis* (Boston: Allen & Unwin).

Pang, X., Zhu, Z., Xu, F., Guo, J., Gong, X., Liu, D., Liu, Z., Chin, D.P. and Feikin, D.R. (2003), 'Evaluation of Control Measures Implemented in the Severe Acute Respiratory Syndrome Outbreak in Beijing, 2003', *JAMA* 290, 3215–21.

Parens, E. (2004), 'Genetic Differences and Human Identities: On Why Talking About Behavioral Genetics is Important and Difficult', *Hastings Center Report Special Supplement* 34:1, S1–35.

Pateman, C. (1988), *The Sexual Contract* (Cambridge: Polity).

Pattinson, S. (2002), 'Reproductive Cloning: Can Cloning Harm the Clone?', *Medical Law Review* 10:3, 295–307.

Patrizio, P., Mastroianni, A.C. and Mastroianni, L. (2001), 'Disclosure to Children Conceived with Donor Gametes Should be Optional', *Human Reproduction* 16:10, 2036–8.

Pennings, G. (2002), 'Reproductive Tourism as Moral Pluralism in Motion', *Journal of Medical Ethics* 28:6, 337–41.

—— (2004), 'Legal Harmonization and Reproductive Tourism in Europe', *Human Reproduction* 19:12, 2689–94.

Petchesky, R. (2003), *Global Prescriptions: Gendering Health and Human Rights* (London: Zed Books).

Petersen, K. (2006), 'The Rights of Donor-Conceived Children to Know the Identity of Their Donor: The Problem of the Known Unknowns and the Unknown Unknowns', in B. Bennett and G.F. Tomossy (eds), *Globalization and Health: Challenges for Health Law and Bioethics* (Dordrecht: Springer), 151–67.

Phelan, D. (1992), 'Right to Life of the Unborn v. Promotion of Trade in Services: The European Court of Justice and the Normative Shaping of the European Union', *Modern Law Review* 55:5, 670–89.

Porter, R. (1997), *The Greatest Benefit to Mankind: A Medical History of Humanity* (New York: W.W. Norton and Company).

Poutanen, S.M., Low, D.E., Henry, B., Finkelstein, S., Rose, D., Green, K., Tellier, R., Draker, R., Adachi, D., Ayers, M., Chan, A.K., Skowronski, D.M., Salit, I., Simor, A.E., Slutsky, A.S., Doyle, P.W., Krajden, M., Petric, M., Brunham, R.C., McGeer, A.J. and the Canadian Severe Acute Respiratory Syndrome Study Team (2003), 'Identification of Severe Acute Respiratory Syndrome in Canada', *New England Journal of Medicine* 348, 1995–2005.

President's Council on Bioethics (2002), *Human Cloning and Human Dignity: An Ethical Inquiry* (Washington, DC: President's Council on Bioethics).

—— (2003), *Beyond Therapy: Biotechnology and the Pursuit of Happiness* (Washington, DC: President's Council on Bioethics).

Reid, L. (2005), 'Diminishing Returns? Risk and the Duty to Care in the SARS Epidemic', *Bioethics* 19:4, 348–61.

Resnik, D. (2001), 'Developing Drugs for the Developing World: An Economic, Legal, Moral and Political Dilemma', *Developing World Bioethics* 1:1, 11–32.

—— (2004), 'The Distribution of Biomedical Research Resources and International Justice', *Developing World Bioethics* 4:1, 42–57.

Reynolds, C. (2004), *Public Health Law and Regulation* (Annandale, NSW: Federation Press).

Rhoden, N. (1987), 'Cesareans and Samaritans', *Law, Medicine & Health Care* 15:3, 118–25.

Ries, N. (2005), 'Quarantine and the Law: The 2003 SARS Experience in Canada (A New Disease Calls on Old Public Health Tools)', *Alberta Law Review* 43:2, 529–47.

Roach Anleu, S. (1990), 'New Procreative Technologies, Donor Gametes and the Law's Response: Developments in Australia', *Australian Journal of Social Issues* 25, 40–51.

—— (1997), 'Reproductive Autonomy and Reproductive Technology: Gender, Deviance and Infertility', in K Petersen (ed.), *Intersections: Women on Law, Medicine and Technology* (Aldershot: Ashgate), 99–125.

Roberts, D. (1995), 'The Genetic Tie', *University of Chicago Law Review* 62:1, 209–73.

Robertson, J. (1994), *Children of Choice: Freedom and the New Reproductive Technologies* (Princeton, NJ: Princeton University Press).

—— (2003), 'Procreative Liberty in the Era of Genomics', *American Journal of Law and Medicine* 29, 439–87.

Robertson, R. (1995), 'Glocalization: Time-Space and Homogeneity-Heterogeneity', in M. Featherstone, S. Lash and R. Robertson (eds), *Global Modernities* (London and Thousand Oaks, CA: Sage Publications), 25–44.

Rogers, W. (2006), 'Feminism and Public Health Ethics', *Journal of Medical Ethics* 32, 351–4.

Rothschild, J. (2005), *The Dream of the Perfect Child* (Bloomington: Indiana University Press).

Rowland, R. (1992), *Living Laboratories: Women and Reproductive Technologies* (Sydney: Sun Books).

Salter, B. and Jones, M. (2002), 'Regulating Human Genetics: The Changing Politics of Biotechnology Governance in the European Union', *Health, Risk & Society* 4:3, 325–40.

Sandelowski, M. (1990), 'Fault Lines: Infertility and Imperiled Sisterhood', *Feminist Studies* 16, 33–51.

Saul, J.R. (2005), *The Collapse of Globalism and the Reinvention of the World* (Toronto: Viking Canada).

Savulescu, J. (1999), 'Sex Selection: The Case For', *Medical Journal of Australia* 171, 373–5.

—— (2001), 'Procreative Beneficence: Why We Should Select the Best Children', *Bioethics* 15:5–6, 413–26.

Scheper-Hughes, N. (2003), 'Keeping an Eye on the Global Traffic in Human Organs', *Lancet* 361, 1645–8.

Schüklenk, U. and Ashcroft, R. (2000), 'International Research Ethics', *Bioethics* 14:2, 158–72.

Scott, M.L., Whelan, A., Dewdney, J. and Zwi, A.B. (2004), '"Brain Drain" or Ethical Recruitment? Solving Health Workforce Shortages With Professionals from Developing Countries', *Medical Journal of Australia* 180, 174–6.

Scott, R. (2000), 'Maternal Duties Toward the Unborn: Soundings from the Law of Torts', *Medical Law Review* 8, 1–68.

—— (2005), 'The Uncertain Scope of Reproductive Autonomy in Preimplantation Genetic Diagnosis and Selective Abortion', *Medical Law Review* 13, 291–327.

—— (2006), 'Choosing Between Possible Lives: Legal and Ethical Issues in Preimplantation Genetic Diagnosis', *Oxford Journal of Legal Studies* 26, 153–78.

Selgelid, M. (2005), 'Ethics and Infectious Disease', *Bioethics* 19:3, 273–89.

Senate Select Committee on the Human Embryo Experimentation Bill 1985 (1986), *Human Embryo Experimentation in Australia* (Canberra: Australian Government Publishing Service).

Serneels, P., Lindelöw, M., Garcia-Montalvo, J. and Barr, A. (2005), 'For Public Service or Money: Understanding Geographical Imbalances in the Health Workforce' (World Bank Policy Research Working Paper No. 3686, August 2005).

Shanin, E. (2002), 'International Response to Human Cloning', *Chicago Journal of International Law* 3:1, 255–61.

Shapiro, M. (2002), 'Does Technological Enhancement of Human Traits Threaten Human Equality and Democracy?', *San Diego Law Review* 39, 769–842.

Sheldon, S. (2005), 'Fragmenting Fatherhood: The Regulation of Reproductive Technologies', *Modern Law Review* 68:4, 523–53.

—— and Thomson, M. (eds) (1998), *Feminist Perspectives on Health Care Law* (London: Cavendish Publishing).

Sheldon, S. and Wilkinson, S. (2001), 'Termination of Pregnancy for Reason of Foetal Disability: Are There Grounds for a Special Exception in Law?', *Medical Law Review* 9, 85–109.

—— (2004), 'Hashmi and Whitaker: An Unjustifiable and Misguided Distinction?', *Medical Law Review* 12:2, 137–63.

Sidel, R. (2006), *Unsung Heroines: Single Mothers and the American Dream* (Berkeley: University of California Press).

Smart, C. (1987), '"There Is Of Course the Distinction Dictated by Nature": Law and the Problem of Paternity', in M. Stanworth (ed.), *Reproductive Technologies: Gender, Motherhood and Medicine* (Minneapolis: University of Minnesota Press), 98–117.

Smith, G.P. (2006), 'Law, Religion and Medicine: Conjunctive or Disjunctive?', *Macquarie Law Symposium* 3, 9–39.

Somerville, M. (1982), 'Birth Technology, Parenting and "Deviance"', *International Journal of Law and Psychiatry* 5, 123–53.

South Australian Council on Reproductive Technology (2000a), *Annual Report 2000* (Adelaide: Department of Human Services).

—— (2000b), *Conception by Donation: Access to Identifying Information in the Use of Donated Sperm, Eggs and Embryos in Reproductive Technology in South Australia.* Discussion Paper of the South Australian Council on Reproductive Technology (Adelaide: South Australian Council on Reproductive Technology).

Spriggs, M. and Savulescu, J. (2002), 'Saviour Siblings', *Journal of Medical Ethics* 28, 289.

Steele, J. (2004), *Risks and Legal Theory* (Oxford: Hart Publishing).

Stock, G. (2002), *Redesigning Humans: Our Inevitable Genetic Future* (Boston and New York: Houghton Mifflin).

Stychin, C. (1998), 'Body Talk: Rethinking Autonomy, Commodification and the Embodied Legal Self', in S. Sheldon and M. Thomson (eds), *Feminist Perspectives on Health Care Law* (London: Cavendish Publishing), 211–36.

Surowiecki, J. (2004), *The Wisdom of Crowds: Why the Many Are Smarter Than the Few and How Collective Wisdom Shapes Business, Economies, Societies and Nations* (New York: Doubleday).

Tangwa, G. (2004), 'Bioethics, Biotechnology and Culture: A Voice From the Margins', *Developing World Bioethics* 4:2, 125–38.

Tarrant, S. (2002), 'State Secrets: Access to Information Under the Human Reproductive Technology Act 1991 (WA)', *Journal of Law and Medicine* 9:3, 336–46.

Thomson, J.J. (1971), 'A Defense of Abortion', *Philosophy and Public Affairs* 1:1, 47–66.

Tobin, J. (2004), *The* Convention on the Rights of the Child*: The Rights and Best Interests of Children Conceived Through Assisted Reproduction* (Melbourne: Victorian Law Reform Commission).

Tsang, K.W., Ho, P.L., Ooi, G.C., Yee, W.K., Wang, T., Chan-Yeung, M., Lam, W.K., Seto, W.H., Yam, L.Y., Cheung, T.M., Wong, P.C., Lam, B., Ip, M.S., Chan, J., Yuen, K.Y. and Lai, K.N. (2003), 'Cluster of Cases of Severe Acute Respiratory Syndrome in Hong Kong', *New England Journal of Medicine* 348, 1977–85.

Tutton, R. (2004), '"They Want to Know Where They Came From": Population Genetics, Identity and Family Genealogy', *New Genetics and Society* 23:1, 105–20.

UNESCO (United Nations Educational, Scientific and Cultural Organization) (2002), *Report of the IBC on Ethics, Intellectual Property and Genomics* (Paris: United Nations Educational, Scientific and Cultural Organisation).

Verlinksy, Y., Rechitsky, S., Schoolcraft, W., Strom, C. and Kuliev, A. (2001), 'Preimplantation Diagnosis for Fanconi Anemia Combined with HLA Matching', *Journal of the American Medical Association* 285, 3130–33.

Verlinksy, Y., Rechitsky, S., Sharapova, T., Morris, R., Taranissi, M. and Kuliev, A. (2004), 'Preimplantation HLA Testing', *Journal of the American Medical Association* 291, 2079–85.

Verlinksy, Y., Rechitsky, S., Verlinsky, O., Masciangelo, C., Lederer, K. and Kuliev, A. (2002), 'Preimplantation Diagnosis for Early-Onset Alzheimer Disease Caused by V717L Mutation', *Journal of the American Medical Association* 287:8, 1018–21.

Victorian Law Reform Commission (2005a), *Assisted Reproductive Technology & Adoption: Position Paper Two: Parentage* (Melbourne: Victorian Law Reform Commission).

—— (2005b), *Assisted Reproductive Technology and Adoption: Position Paper Three: Surrogacy* (Melbourne: Victorian Law Reform Commission).

—— (2007), *Assisted Reproductive Technology and Adoption: Final Report* (Melbourne: Victorian Law Reform Commission).

Walker, K. (2002), 'Should There Be Limits on Who May Access Assisted Reproductive Services?', *Flinders Journal of Law Reform* 6:1, 67–93.

Waller Committee – see Committee to Consider the Social, Ethical and Legal Issues Arising from In Vitro Fertilisation.

Waller, L. (1998), 'Regulating Birth Technology', *Res Publica* 7:3, 18–24.

Wang, Y.A., Dean, J.H., Grayson, N. and Sullivan, A.E. (2006), *Assisted Reproduction Technology in Australia and New Zealand 2004.* Assisted Reproduction Technology Series No. 10. Cat. No. PER39 (Sydney: AIHW National Perinatal Statistics Unit).

Warnock, M. (1984), *Report of the Committee of Inquiry Into Human Fertilisation and Embryology* (Cmnd 9314, London: HMSO).

Watson, J. (2004), *DNA: The Secret of Life* (London: Arrow Books).

Wilkinson, S. (2003), *Bodies for Sale: Ethics and Exploitation in the Human Body Trade* (London: Routledge).

Williams, P. (1991), *The Alchemy of Race and Rights* (Cambridge, MA: Harvard University Press).

Wolf, S.M. (1994), 'Shifting Paradigms in Bioethics and Health Law: The Rise of a New Pragmatism', *American Journal of Law and Medicine* 20:4, 395–415.

World Health Assembly (2004), *Human Organ and Tissue Transplantation* (Resolution WHA57.18, 22 May 2004).

World Health Organisation (2002a), *Genomics and World Health: Report of the Advisory Committee on Health Research* (Geneva: World Health Organisation).

—— (2002b), *Global Crises – Global Solutions: Managing Public Health Emergencies of International Concern Through the Revised International Health Regulations* (Geneva: World Health Organisation).

—— (2003a), *Severe Acute Respiratory Syndrome (SARS): Status of the Outbreak and Lessons for the Immediate Future* (Geneva: World Health Organisation).

—— (2003b), *Update 96 – Taiwan, China: SARS Transmission Interrupted in Last Outbreak Area* <http://www.who.int/csr/don/2003_07_05/en/>, accessed 20 March 2007.

—— (2003c), *Summary of Probable SARS Cases With Onset of Illness from 1 November 2002 to 31 July 2003* (revised 26 September 2003) <http://www.who.int/csr/sars/country/table2003_09_23/en/>, accessed 20 March 2007.

—— (2004), *World Health Report 2004: Changing History* (Geneva: World Health Organisation).

—— (2005a), *Plague: Fact Sheet No. 267*, revised February 2005 <http://www.who.int/mediacentre/factsheets/fs267/en/index.html>, accessed 20 March 2007.

—— (2005b), *Avian Influenza: Assessing the Pandemic Threat* (Geneva: World Health Organisation).

—— (2005c), *Strengthening Pandemic Influenza Preparedness and Response – Report by the Secretariat* (58th World Health Assembly A58/13).

—— (2005d), *Impact of Plague* <http://www.who.int/csr/disease/plague/impact/en/index.html>, accessed 20 March 2007.

—— (2006), *Working Together for Health: The World Health Report 2006* (Geneva: World Health Organisation).

—— (2007), *Cumulative Number of Confirmed Human Cases of Avian Influenza A/(H5N1) Reported to WHO* (published online) <http://www.who.int/csr/disease/avian_influenza?country/cases_table_2007_12_04/en/index.html>, accessed 7 December 2007.

World Health Organisation Writing Group (2006a), 'Nonpharmaceutical Interventions for Pandemic Influenza, International Measures', *Emerging Infectious Diseases* 12:1, 81–7.

—— (2006b), 'Nonpharmaceutical Interventions for Pandemic Influenza, National and Community Measures', *Emerging Infectious Diseases* 12:1, 88–94.

Wu, Z., Viisainen, K. and Hemminki, E. (2006), 'Determinants of High Sex Ratio Among Newborns: A Cohort Study from Rural Anhui Province, China', *Reproductive Health Matters* 14:27, 172–80.

Index